July 27, 1989

To Mintadg, our very special friend—

Congratulations on your American Citizenship. This book seemed perfect ... all the beautiful things that make America special ... You are one of them.

Love,
Cookie and Warren

AMERICA

Text by Marvin Karp

Editor
Gillian Waugh

Designer
Philip Clucas MSIAD

Production Director
Gerald Hughes

Editorial Director
David Gibbon

Publishing Director
Ted Smart

CLB 1688
Copyright © 1987 Colour Library Books Ltd.,
    Guildford, Surrey, England.
Printed and bound in Barcelona, Spain by Cronion, S.A.

Published 1987 by Portland House
Distributed by Crown Publishers, Inc.
ISBN 0 517 63394 9
h g f e d c b a

AMERICA

Foreword by
GERALD R. FORD

Text by
MARVIN KARP

PORTLAND HOUSE

Foreword

It stretches from within a shiver of the Arctic Circle almost to the balmy Tropics. Its seacoasts range from dramatic cliffs to gentle sand dunes. It has mountains of every description, from ancient rolling hills to young rocky peaks. It has vast stretches of desert and places where the rain averages more than an inch a week. It has some of the largest lakes in the world, and some of the longest rivers. It has more than its share of record-breaking waterfalls and nearly 75 percent of the world's active volcanoes.

It is home to nearly 239 million souls, most of whom are proud to call themselves "Americans." They live in natural environments that are the envy of the world and in cities and towns that the whole world emulates. They share their space with some 750 species of trees, more different kinds of animals than roam the African continent and more species of birds than fly over any other single landmass on earth.

Yet, though the American continent has been home to the human race since the end of the ice age, it was unknown to the civilized world until 500 years ago, and it wasn't until 300 years ago that Europeans decided it might be a nice place to live.

By that time Niagara Falls had already carved a gorge several miles long, the Colorado River had cut a canyon a mile deep and the Mississippi River had built a delta of well over 10,000 square miles. The biggest volcano on earth had exploded and created a lake six miles across and a half mile deep. Geysers at the edge of the Rocky Mountains were spewing steam and hot water into the air and trees growing in the moist air of the Pacific Coast mountains already soared more than 300 feet into the air.

But in spite of all that, the people who began arriving from Europe in the 17th century began changing things from the moment they stepped off the boat. Following the lead of the Indians who preceeded them, they built fires to clear the forests, but they had better tools and bigger dreams and accelerated the pace. In no time at all they had fenced-in towns with parks in the center and church steeples overlooking a landscape they themselves had created. Before much longer, they widened the Indian trails to connect their towns and in less than 100 years managed to make the land as worn out as the farms they had left behind in the Old Country. But there was plenty of new country out there, and not long after they declared themselves a New Nation, a third of all Americans lived west of the Allegheny Mountains. And every one of them was hard at work altering the landscape.

But in spite of what's been done to change it, America is still one of the natural wonders of the world, still rich in all the ways man measures such things, from mineral resources to productive farms. It is rich in natural beauty, too. Nothing quite compares to an autumn afternoon in New England, or a thunderstorm on the prairie. Nothing is quite the same as a starry evening on the plains of Texas, except possibly a stroll down Broadway in the City of New York. All of it is America. Nothing like it exists anywhere else.

Gerald R. Ford

GERALD R. FORD

"When in the Course of human events it becomes necessary for one people to dissolve the political bonds which have connected them with another, and to assume among the powers of earth, the separate and equal station to which the Laws of Nature and Nature's God entitle them, a decent respect to the opinions of mankind requires that they should declare the causes which impel them to the separation...

"We hold these truths to be self-evident, that all men are created equal, that they are endowed by their Creator with certain unalienable Rights, that among these are Life, Liberty and the pursuit of Happiness..."

This is the preamble to one of the most simply stated yet stirring documents on human rights ever written: the Declaration of Independence. And when representatives of the 13 British colonies in America appended their signatures to it, they became, at one and the same time, treasonous rebels and Founding Fathers. For this document, adopted by the Second Continental Congress in Philadelphia on July 4, 1776, placed the 13 colonies in open rebellion against the mother country. It also announced the birth of a new nation – the United States of America.

The decision to break with England was not made in haste but had been gathering momentum for many years. The colonies had long resented the subservient role and harsh taxation policies imposed on them, and tried, to no avail, to have the Crown modify or ease them. Though many of the colonies were as dissimilar as any neighboring countries in the Old World, their antipathy to British rule finally became strong enough to unite them against the common enemy. By the time they formally declared their intention of becoming independent, their resentment had already turned to open resistance. On April 19, 1775, Colonial Minutemen faced British Redcoats at Lexington and Concord, Massachusetts. The first shots of the Revolution were fired, and the first blood shed. The spirit of independence, and the willingness to do whatever was necessary to sustain it, had emerged as an integral part of the American ethos and character.

But none of this might ever have come to pass had it not been for an independent-thinking and determined Italian navigator who, flying the flag of Spain, followed his dream into the setting sun, and discovered a new world. Christopher Columbus, a seasoned navigator from Genoa, believed that by sailing westward he would not, contrary to popular belief, fall off the edge of the earth, but instead find the shortest way to the riches of the Orient. At that time, most of the trade with India, China and Japan was conducted along tortuous overland routes established long before by the Crusaders and Marco Polo. For almost ten years, Columbus had petitioned the crowned heads of several European countries for funds to outfit a sea-going expedition to prove his theory, with no success.

Then, in 1487, a significant breakthrough occurred when a Portuguese captain, Bartholomew Diaz, sailed around the southernmost tip of Africa and then east to the Orient. Goaded by the success of her tiny neighbor, Portugal, in opening up a new all-water trade route, Queen Isabella of Spain decided to invest in Columbus' dream. That investment, estimated at about $14,000, was destined to bring Spain incalculable wealth, and a whole new world to rule. But that was all still in the future when on August 3, 1492, three small ships, the *Santa Maria*, the *Nina* and the *Pinta*, sailed with the tide from the harbor of Palos, Spain, under the command of Christopher Columbus. Destination: the Indies.

Surviving uncharted seas, a near-mutiny and the longest voyage anyone had ever made out of sight of land, the fleet came upon a tiny island in what is now known as the Bahamas in the early morning hours of October 12. When Columbus and his crew planted the Spanish flag on the island and named it San Salvador, they became the first Europeans on record to set foot on land in the Western Hemisphere, though it has been said that some Norsemen actually reached the coast of North America as early as the year 1,000 A.D.

In commemoration of Columbus' feat, October 12 has been celebrated as a legal holiday throughout the United States since 1920. The first Columbus Day celebration took place in 1792 on the 300th anniversary of the discovery. It was not celebrated again until the 400th anniversary in 1892.

Convinced that San Salvador (now also known as Watling Island), plus a large island he named Hispaniola (Little Spain) and others he encountered were lying off the coast of the Indies, Columbus called the area the "West Indies", and the inhabitants "Indians". He also mistakenly thought that Cuba was part of China.

Columbus made three more journeys of colonization and exploration, and with each one he ventured further and further across the water until he touched several parts of Central America and eventually the northeast coast of South America, never knowing that his quest was doomed to fail because of the land mass blocking his way. In fact, it was not until 1519-20, some years after the death of Columbus that Ferdinand Magellan, a Portuguese navigator in the service of Spain, found a passage to the Orient by sailing around the southern tip of South America and into the Pacific Ocean.

Christopher Columbus died on May 20, 1506, in the Spanish town of Valladolid, unacclaimed, virtually impoverished, and probably unaware of the magnitude of the contribution he had made to the world and to history. And his accomplishment was destined to be clouded further when by a quirk of fate a German geographer gave the New World the name "America" under the mistaken impression that it had been discovered by the Florentine navigator, Amerigo Vespucci.

During the 16th century, Spain was the country that initially gained the most from Columbus' exploits. Armed expeditions were sent to Mexico, Central and South America where they found thriving civilizations among the Mayan, Aztec and Incan peoples. But, more than that, the Conquistadores found gold, silver and precious gems beyond their greatest expectations. Being more interested in conquering than colonizing, the invaders used their superior firepower to defeat and enslave the local populace while plundering the land. Soon, huge fleets of Spanish ships were carrying treasures back to the homeland on a regular basis.

Curiously, not too much attention was being paid to the North American continent. Exploratory probes were sent out by the English, Dutch and French as well as the Spaniards in the hopes of finding a northwest passage to India. Besides the establishment of St Augustine in

Florida by Spain in 1565, no other attempt at a permanent settlement was made by any European power until almost the end of the century. The English appeared to be more predisposed to privateering on Spanish treasure galleons and Spanish ports in the New World, than the commercial possibilities of colonization. Other countries found that their citizens were reluctant to trade the comforts of their homes for the uncertainties of life in a wilderness.

ROANOKE ISLAND

The first serious attempts at colonization by the British were sponsored by Sir Walter Raleigh – soldier, explorer, privateer and favorite of Queen Elizabeth I. He underwrote an expedition in 1584 that explored the coast of North America from what is now the state of North Carolina down to Florida. Raleigh named the area Virginia, in honor of the Virgin Queen and sent out another expedition with over 100 colonists, all men, the following year. Their mission: to establish a permanent settlement on Roanoke Island. But their inability to cope with the wilderness, plus sickness and fear took a heavy toll and caused the survivors to return to England **within** a year aboard the ships of Sir Francis Drake, who **had stopped** there to check on the colony.

In 1587, Raleigh sent out another group of colonists, comprised of 91 men, 17 women and 9 children, under the leadership of John White. Soon after their arrival at Roanoke, the colony's population was increased by another arrival, a baby girl. The daughter of Ananias Dare and Ellinor White, she was named Virginia Dare and was the first English child to be born in the New World. But that may have been the last happy event to take place in the luckless settlement.

John White, who was the grandfather of the infant as well as the expedition's leader, then returned to England for much-needed supplies. Unfortunately, he was trapped at home when Philip of Spain sent his Armada to conquer England in 1588. Thus, it was not until 1591 that John White returned with the supplies only to find the settlement abandoned and no sign of the colonists. No trace of them was ever found. The only clue they left behind was a single word carved in the trunk of a tree. That word was "Croatan".

The only material benefits accrued from the Roanoke Island failures appear to have been the white potato, which Sir Ralph Lane, governor of the first short-lived colony, introduced to his Irish estate, and the second was tobacco, which Raleigh popularized by smoking the brown leaf.

Despite the unsuccessful attempts to colonize Roanoke Island, the idea of establishing English settlements on the American continent had taken hold. It was also realized that sponsoring and maintaining such an undertaking were beyond the financial abilities of any one person. It required the backing of either the Crown or a well-funded organization, like a corporation.

When James I acceded to the English throne, he opted for the corporate approach and issued charters to two groups of merchants authorizing the establishment of two settlements, each comprised of 10,000 square miles. The London Company was assigned the area between the 34th and 41st parallels. The Plymouth Company's territory lay to the north between the 38th and 45th parallels.

The charters stipulated that a council, appointed by the king and sitting in England, would supervise the overall management of each colony. It would, in turn, appoint a local council to conduct day-to-day affairs in America. This colonial council was to be self-governing, but it had to comply with English Law and could not pass any laws of its own affecting life and limb.

JAMESTOWN, VIRGINIA

When the London Company offered shares in its Virginia colonizing venture, hundreds of Englishmen eagerly subscribed to what they believed would be a get-rich-quick opportunity. The money went to outfit a small fleet, and on December 20, 1606, the *Susan Constant, Godspeed* and *Discovery*, commanded by Captain Christopher Newport, sailed down the Thames bound for Virginia. On board were 104 emigrants (100 men and 4 boys) whose primary interest was to search for gold and other treasure.

Five months later, the ships arrived at Chesapeake Bay, sailed up the James River for about 60 miles and dropped anchor off a little peninsula on May 14. The colonists went ashore and established their settlement, naming it and the river in honor of King James. Unfortunately, the site for Jamestown turned out to be the first in a series of disasters that almost wiped out the fledgling colony. The settlement was located on swampy ground, with an impure water supply, which caused many of the men to contract malaria, dysentery and pneumonia.

It soon became apparent that few of the colonists had the skills, knowledge or interest to survive for any length of time in the wilderness. They had made the trip to find a hoard of gold, such as the Spaniards had discovered, and take it back to England. But, there was no gold, no treasure waiting to be gathered, only sickness, dwindling food supplies and discontent. Had it not been for the discipline and determination of Captain John Smith, the colony would have perished that first winter.

Smith drove them to build shelters. He bartered with the Indians for corn and other food, and survived being captured by Powhatan, chief of the 30-tribe Indian confederacy in Virginia. It was Pocahontas, the chief's daughter, who saved Smith from execution. Several years later, she married John Rolfe, one of the colonists, which led to a temporary peace between the Indians and the settlers.

When Smith returned to England for treatment of wounds he had sustained in an accident, the colony reached its nadir. Without sufficient supplies to last out the winter of 1609-10 and fearful of being ambushed by the Indians, the residents of Jamestown endured what was later called "the starving time". They ate anything they could find nearby, including snakes, rats, mice and roots. They also burned the timbers of their houses rather than risk venturing into the forest for firewood.

By the time a relief expedition arrived in May, 1610, Jamestown had been reduced to a handful of survivors who wanted nothing more than to go back to England. But along with fresh supplies and a new contingent of settlers, a new governor, Thomas West (Lord De La Warr), arrived bringing with him a new charter from the Virginia Company that offered residents stock incentives for which they could pay with their labor. Now, the colonists could earn a permanent stake in the New World by settling down to farming and developing local industries and products.

The first important result of the new policy occurred when John Rolfe introduced tobacco seeds from Trinidad that produced a sweeter leaf than the native Virginia leaf and was more readily saleable. Within two years, tobacco farming blossomed to the point where Jamestown was exporting roughly $8 million worth of produce to England. To encourage more colonization and increased production of other farm crops, the Company charter was further amended so that land could be offered as an incentive to potential colonists. This proved to be a great success, and new settlements literally sprouted around Jamestown.

The year 1619 proved to be a landmark for both Jamestown and the foundation of a nation yet to come, with three important events taking place in the space of twelve months. On August 9, the first representative assembly met in the church in Jamestown. This assembly, called the House of Burgesses, included the Governor, George Yeardley, his Council and 22 burgesses, two elected from each of the nearby settlements. The purpose of the meeting was to make new laws for the colony. From that day on, Virginia was essentially self-governing though the government of England had veto power over laws it considered unfavorable. That assembly became the model for many of the law-making bodies that later formed the basis of self-government throughout the United States. It was a vital first step in the democratic process.

The next event of consequence was the arrival at Jamestown of a Dutch ship carrying 20 blacks who were sold into bondage as servants, marking the beginning of slavery in the American South.

The third occurrence was the arrival of a boatload of "young, handsome and honestly educated maids", sent by the Company to become wives for the colony's bachelors. It was the Company's intention to promote the development of a stable environment in the community and a feeling of permanence in the colony.

Three years later, following the death of Chief Powhatan, his successor broke the peace on Good Friday and killed several hundred colonists. The colony was too well-established, however, to be destroyed then, or in subsequent Indian attacks. From that date on, a state of war existed between the colonists and the Indians.

In 1676, Jamestown was burned to the ground when Nathaniel Bacon, a planter, led a rebellion against the royal governor (the Crown had taken over Virginia as a royal colony in 1624). It was burned again in 1698, and this time the Virginians transferred their capital to Williamsburg rather than rebuild Jamestown again.

NEW ENGLAND

The Pilgrims
Captain John Smith was not only responsible for saving the Jamestown colony from extinction during its first desperate winter, he undoubtedly played an unintentional but important role in the establishment of the second permanent English settlement in America.

Recovered from the injuries that had forced him to return to England, Smith was hired in 1614 by some London merchants to lead a whaling expedition along the coast of North America. This gave him an opportunity to explore the area, which he later recounted in a book entitled *A Description of New England*.

Smith's book created such interest and excitement in England that it became the 17th century equivalent of a best seller. Some merchant members of the London Company, sensing that the time might be right to set up another permanent colony in the New World, obtained a royal patent for the region that lay between the 40th and 48th parallels and extended from sea to sea. The next step was to recruit the potential colonists. As the fates would have it, there was a ready-made group of people in Holland who were looking for a new place to live.

Several years earlier, a contingent of religious dissenters left England to live in Leyden, Holland, in order to avoid persecution for breaking away from the Anglican Church. These people, known as Separatists, had a difficult time adjusting to life among the Dutch and were willing to move once again. When the London Company offered them passage, land in America and a chance to worship in their own way, they accepted.

Returning to England, they found a ship, the *Mayflower*, waiting for them at Plymouth, along with another party of eager emigrants whom they called the Strangers. The latter group were not religious refugees; they were members of the Church of England who looked to America as a place where they could have their own land and improve their lot in life. On September 16, 1620, the *Mayflower* weighed anchor and headed out to sea carrying a boatload of Pilgrims (40 Separatists, 62 Strangers) and the makings of an explosive situation.

Once at sea, it quickly became apparent that the Separatists were no more tolerant of the Anglicans than the Church of England had been of them. Friction between the two groups, foul weather and close quarters brought emotions to the edge of violence as the tiny ship battled through the rough seas. Then, on the 65th day, as a conflict seemed unavoidable, the *Mayflower* dropped anchor in Provincetown Harbor, just inside the tip of Cape Cod. By a rapid reckoning, the passengers realized that they were far north of their designated landing site, so far north, in fact, that they were beyond the territorial limit of the London Company's patent. It was now November 21, and rather than risk facing the heavy seas again, the weary travelers decided to settle in the area.

To preserve the unity of the infant colony and create some guidelines for the common good, the Pilgrim leaders drew up the now-famous Mayflower Compact, the first plan for self-determining government ever devised and enacted in America. Under this document, which was signed by all 41 male adult members of both groups, Separatists and Strangers agreed to form a government and to be ruled by "just and equal laws" formulated by that government. Then, in the first free election ever held on these shores, they chose Deacon John Carver as the first Colonial Governor in the New World.

Because of inclement weather, it took the scouting parties until December 21 to find a suitable site for the settlement. Five days later, the rest of the colonists landed at the place they called Plymouth and began throwing up crude huts and shelters to protect themselves from the bitter climate. Sickness, lack of proper food and bad weather combined to ravage the ranks of the settlers, and by spring half of them were dead. But for the survivors, a happy surprise occurred one March day when an Indian named Samoset walked into the village and introduced himself. He returned two weeks later with another Indian named Squanto, who, in the ensuing months, taught the colonists how to increase the productivity of their fields and how to hunt and fish.

Later that spring, the colonists and the Indians, under Chief Massasoit, signed a peace treaty and set up a fur trade. By autumn, Plymouth was so well-established that William Bradford, who became governor on John Carver's death, declared a three-day festival and invited their Indian friends to join the first Thanksgiving celebration.

The colony continued to thrive and grow as new settlers arrived from England. By 1627, the inhabitants were able to buy up their obligations to the London Company for £1,800 and free themselves of financial control from England.

The Puritans
The Separatists were not the only group opposed to the conduct of the Church of England, but the other protestants wanted to bring about reforms by working within the Church rather than breaking away. Their objective was to "purify" the Church of its pomp, ceremony and power, hence the name "Puritans".

Heartened by the success of the Plymouth colony and the several smaller settlements that spun off from it, a group of Puritans, under the leadership of John Winthrop, applied for and received a charter from King Charles I to establish their own colony. The grant, issued in 1629 to the Massachusetts Bay Company, added another significant facet to the development of American democracy just as the Mayflower Compact did. In this case, the charter gave the Puritans the right to govern themselves in America without a council in England to oversee or supervise them.

At first, a group of 300 Puritans, led by John Endecott, joined a three-year-old settlement of Pilgrims at Salem, but left the following year to found their own community near present-day Boston. They were joined soon after by another group of Puritans led by John Winthrop.

The unaccustomed rigors of wilderness life had such a debilitating effect that the settlers appealed in desperation to the Plymouth Colony for medical assistance. The Pilgrims not only treated their physical problems but their spiritual ones as well. They persuaded the Puritans to break completely with the Church of England and adopt the tenets of the Pilgrim Church. This meant that every congregation was to be self-governing, with members electing the pastor and other officers. Community and religious life, interrelated and based around the meeting house, were to be stripped of all ceremony, reverting to the simple ways of Biblical days when the Scripture was the only law. All of this was promulgated in the name of democratic equalitarianism, a worthy concept that was preached but not really practiced. For instance, the Pilgrim/Puritans were totally intolerant of any other religion being practiced in their communities, which later caused some members to be banished or to desert the colony for other locales.

Meanwhile, England was going through a period of unrest and discontent under the rule of Charles I. This brought on a wave of migration to America, primarily to the Bay Colony area. By 1640, there were about 10,000 settlers in and around Boston, a larger number than the entire population of all the other English/American colonies. As the Bay Colony continued to grow and the colonists moved outward to form new settlements, their Indian friends became more and more apprehensive about the increasing encroachment on their homelands.

The first real trouble erupted as early as 1636 in the area that became known as Connecticut, when settlers from Massachusetts began to farm on land owned by the Pequot Indians. Fighting resulted in several hundred Indians being burned alive or killed as they tried to escape, and the remainder of the tribe sold into slavery in the West Indies.

Another outcome of that bloody affair was the formation by the colonists of the Confederation of New England for mutual protection. This was the first attempt at a confederacy of colonies in the New World, and though it only lasted for 20 years, it served as a lesson in cooperation that would have an impact on American history more than 100 years later.

The second major Indian uprising took place in 1675 when King Philip, son of Chief Massasoit, tried to drive the white settlers out of New England. Though the colonists killed Philip in a battle on August 6, 1676, the war continued for two more years. By the time the Indians were defeated, they had killed more than 1,000 settlers and destroyed a dozen towns. All this time the colonists still lived in fear of the Spaniards, who claimed the entire New World for themselves and enforced the policy of 'no peace beyond the line' until the end of the century.

Although the Massachusetts colonists enjoyed a great deal of freedom from interference by the King or Parliament, they were still bound by the terms of the charter granted by Charles I. And when they refused to restrict their trade to only the mother country, Charles II cancelled the charter in 1684. His successor, James II, then established one government for all the northern colonies that he called the Dominion of New England. This was revoked by William and Mary in 1691 when they granted a new charter that combined the Plymouth Colony with the Massachusetts Bay Colony plus the island of Martha's Vineyard, and made them all into a Royal Colony. The following year, Sir William Phips became the first royal governor of Massachusetts, marking the end, temporarily, of the experiment in limited democracy.

RHODE ISLAND

The first genuine apostle of complete religious and political freedom was an English Clergyman named Roger Williams, and the colony he founded became the first real example of true democracy in action. In fact, much of what Williams advocated was later incorporated in the Constitution of the United States.

Because of his outspoken dissent from the Anglican Church, Williams was forced to flee England, arriving at Boston in early 1631. Spurning a post as minister of a Boston church because it was not separatist enough, he became minister of a church in Salem. But Williams soon found himself at odds with the church and the community for speaking out against religious intolerance and social injustice.

He believed it was the privilege of the individual to worship God in his or her own way and not to have to endure religious regimentation. He believed that government and religion should be separate functions, unrelated and independent of each other. He believed that since government is a compact created by the people, it must be responsible to the people and be changed whenever they wish. He believed that every individual has certain rights by natural law. And finally, he believed that the colonists had violated the rights of the Indians by taking their land without permission or payment.

For spreading these "newe and dangerous opinions against the authoritie of magistrates", the Massachusetts General Court ordered that Roger Williams be banished from Massachusetts on September 13, 1635.

Undaunted, Williams led a group of freedom-seeking settlers out of the Bay Colony and across Narraganset Bay to Rhode Island. There he purchased some land from friendly Indian tribes and established the community he called Providence.

Williams set up a system of government that was based on the consent of the citizenry by providing for frequent elections and local home rule. He also created a flexible constitution. Soon, other like-minded colonists were deserting Massachusetts for this haven of democracy, and three new settlements appeared – Portsmouth, Newport and then Warwick. To establish the legitimacy of his colony, Williams obtained a charter from the English Parliamentary Commission in 1644 and brought the four settlements together under its protection. Under the terms of the charter, the colony of Rhode Island gained official recognition, and so did its democratic system of government.

PENNSYLVANIA

In 1644, the year that Roger Williams was in London petitioning for a charter for Rhode Island, a son named William was born to the British naval hero, Admiral Sir William Penn. And as staunch as Roger Williams was in his advocacy of religious tolerance, the rights of the individual and the democratic process, he would be matched by the efforts of young William Penn to bring a new freedom to the New World.

Raised and educated as an aristocrat, William Penn was 16 when he entered Oxford, the same year the Stuart family returned to the throne after the death of Oliver Cromwell. University life did not agree with him, however. Penn found the dress and behavior of the students too affected, but more importantly, he resented the University's rule forcing everyone to attend Church of England services. When he met with other dissident students to protest the lack of religious freedom, he was sent down.

Penn spent the next several years traveling and studying law, and, in 1667, went to Ireland to manage his father's estates. It was then that he met Thomas Loe, a Quaker preacher who completely changed his life.

Shunning a life of complacency and conformity – though he did retain some friends in high places, including the Duke of York, later to become James II – Penn joined the Society of Friends at a time when Quakers were being persecuted and sometimes put to death. In the ensuing years, he, too, was imprisoned several times for writing and preaching Quakerism.

Penn's first involvement in America came about when he was made one of three trustees who were assigned to manage the property of West New Jersey that the Society had acquired as a haven for its members. Towards this end, Penn drew up a charter of "Laws, Concessions, and Agreements" which proclaimed that "no Men, nor number of Men upon Earth, hath Power or Authority to rule over Men's Consciences in religious Matters." This document also guaranteed many "Fundamental Rights" to the settlers concerning their person and property.

Then, in 1681, Charles II paid off a long-standing debt to Penn's father by granting the son a charter for territory in America that lay west of the Delaware River between New York and Maryland. The tract was then named Pennsylvania (Penn's Woods) in honor of the late Admiral. The following year, the Duke of York gave his old friend the additional territory known as Delaware. William Penn now had the place in which to put his beliefs into practice.

Penn envisioned a society comprised of landed gentlemen, like himself, living on great estates, surrounded by free and independent farmers working their own land. He also foresaw people of every faith having the opportunity to worship in peace. He embodied these guarantees of fundamental liberties in a constitution, or "Frame of Government", that he hoped would become the model of a liberal, democratic way of life.

Thousands of colonists from England, Ireland, Germany, Holland and Wales, many of them Quakers, flocked to Pennsylvania and its territory, Delaware. Penn himself made the crossing in 1682 and stayed about two years. During that time, he concluded a peace treaty with the Indians, paying for most of the land he had been given by the Crown. He also initiated the laying out of the city of Philadelphia.

As prescribed by Penn in his constitution, the government of his colonies consisted of a governor (himself), a deputy governor and an elected legislature made up of a provincial council (upper house) and a general assembly (lower house). At first, the power to originate laws rested with the upper house whose appointed delegates represented the landed gentry. The lower house, whose membership was elected, only had the right of approval. When this division of authority proved unworkable, Penn, who had returned to England, came back to the colony and wrote a new constitution which gave greater control of the government to the people. This document, called the Charter of Privileges, made the general assembly the principal lawmaking body, relegating the provincial council to an advisory role.

In 1701, Penn returned to England for the last time. Although he had spent only a total of about four years in America, he made an immeasurable contribution to the future United States. He played a primary part in the establishment of three colonies: Pennsylvania, New Jersey and Delaware. He left a legacy of humanitarian principles that became essential ingredients in the building-blocks of American democracy. But more than that, in his 1693 *Essay towards the Present and Future*, he suggested that an organization like the United Nations be formed to settle international disputes before they led to open hostilities. And four years later, in his *Plan of Union*, he proposed that the English Colonies join together for a common purpose, a plan that became a reality in the next century. William Penn, a man of uncommon conviction and dedication, deserves as much recognition for his contributions to the birth of this country as any of the Founding Fathers.

MARYLAND

Named for Queen Henrietta Maria, wife of England's Charles I, Maryland became the first colony to be founded as a proprietorship since the ill-fated ventures of Sir Walter Raleigh at Roanoke Island. The King granted the charter for a 10,000,000 acre feudal estate to George Calvert, the first Lord Baltimore. When Calvert died before the charter was signed, the title and the grant were passed on to his oldest son, Cecilius, in 1632.

Although the charter granted 'kingly' powers to the Calvert family, Lord Baltimore had no interest in creating a feudal barony. As a Roman Catholic, he wanted a colony where those of his faith could freely worship, and he was willing to accord the same right to people of all faiths. This resulted, some years later, in the Maryland assembly passing an Act Concerning Religion, the first law for religious freedom in the colonies.

As a businessman, Lord Baltimore was more interested in making the colony prosper than exercising the autocratic powers granted to him. To get his colony started, he sponsored two boatloads of settlers, who established St Mary's City near the southern tip of the Western Shore in 1634. Other colonists soon followed, including bands of Puritans from Virginia and other areas, encouraged by the prospect of religious freedom and the promise of acquiring land of their own. Unlike most other colonials, Marylanders never had to undergo the physical and economic tribulations that beset the early settlers. The colony went through some temporary disaffection with the proprietorship, but the population continued to grow as well as the profitability in raising tobacco.

The colony remained in the hands of the Lords Baltimore until the American Revolution, declaring its independence in 1776, but the government became increasingly liberal through the years. Starting with a strong governorship, personally administered during the early years by Leonard Calvert, Lord Baltimore's younger brother, plus a powerless council and a controlled assembly, the government evolved into more of a parliamentary-style organization. The legislature gradually began to assert itself, first assuming the right to convene whenever it saw fit and not just at the whim of the governor. The general assembly then divided into two houses and began to take more responsibility for the initiation as well as the passage of legislation. Just as its sister colonies were discovering, Maryland, too, was learning the lessons of self-government that would stand her in good stead later on.

CAROLINA

When Charles I granted it as a proprietorship to his Attorney General, Sir Robert Heath, in 1629, the area of Carolina (land of Charles) was the largest single piece of unoccupied territory between Virginia and Spanish Florida. Heath made no attempt to colonize it, however, and in 1663, Charles II granted the land to eight of his favorite nobles, making them "Lords Proprietors". These new grantees foolishly tried to reproduce English society in Carolina based on a class system. But since most of the people were emigrating to America to get away from such a system, they expressed their displeasure by revolting against the government. In 1678, they actually replaced the appointed governor with one of their own. And through the year 1689, they forced five governors out of office as they tried to bring about some changes in the government.

The proprietors continued to ignore the colonists' protests and divided the colony in two in order to maintain better control. Then, in 1721, King George I bought back Carolina from the proprietors and granted the colonists more control over their government. Eight years later, he divided the colony into two royal provinces, North and South Carolina, which they remained until the Revolutionary War.

GEORGIA

Last of the original thirteen colonies, and perhaps the most peculiar in its inception, Georgia was lopped off the southern part of South Carolina and set up to create a buffer zone against any northward encroachment by the Spaniards in Florida. King George II granted a charter in 1732 to James Oglethorpe and associates who formed a corporation called Trustees for Establishing the Colony of Georgia in America. The charter stipulated that the trustees would accrue no personal gain from the venture; that the colony would be under strict control of the Crown; and that Georgia would become a royal province after 21 years.

All of those conditions were perfectly acceptable to Oglethorpe because this well-born gentleman and member of Parliament had a special purpose in mind for Georgia. He wanted to use the colony as a way of giving imprisoned and recently released debtors an opportunity to regain a productive place in society. The project was funded by private donations and grants from Parliament. Unfortunately, the plan never quite jelled and very few debtors ever reached these shores.

The Georgia colony was established, however, with Oglethorpe bringing over the first contingent of colonists and setting up the first community near present-day Savannah in February, 1733. Oglethorpe governed the colony well for its first nine years and also soundly defeated a Spanish invasion force, driving the Spaniards back to Florida. By the time the charter expired, Georgia was well-entrenched with more than 4,000 inhabitants. Oglethorpe's humanitarian scheme might have failed, but the colony he organized did not.

To complete the roster of the original 13 colonies requires the addition of Connecticut, New Hampshire and New York. Connecticut was first settled by colonists from Massachusetts seeking greater religious freedom and later received its own charter from England. New Hampshire went through an unsettled early history when initially large tracts of land were awarded to individuals, one of whom – John Mason – named the region after his native county, Hampshire, England. Then the colony was made part of Massachusetts, and finally, it became a royal colony. New York, established by the Dutch as New Amsterdam, was taken over by the British in 1667 and given by Charles II to his brother, the Duke of York (later James II).

With the colonies firmly established, colonial America should have begun to enjoy some of the benefits of the life style that the early settlers had struggled to create. But the struggle was not over. Starting in 1690, and for the next 70 years, the colonies, especially the middle and northern ones, were embroiled in the British/French efforts to dominate the settled and unsettled territories in the New World. The fighting began with the massacre of English colonists at Schenectady, New York, by French and Indian raiders, and did not end until the British had captured Quebec and Montreal. It encompassed four wars – King William's War, Queen Anne's War, King George's War, and the French and Indian War – and destroyed France's colonial dreams.

The Treaty of Paris (1763) gave Canada and all French possessions east of the Mississippi River to Great Britain. Spain, an ally of France during these wars, gave up Florida to Britain, but received, in turn, all French land west of the Mississippi, plus the Isle of Orleans, which included the city of New Orleans. France was allowed to retain two small islands near Newfoundland as unfortified fishing stations, and the Caribbean islands of Guadeloupe and Martinique.

Once its colonial rivals were eliminated, England turned its attention to its American colonies and demanded that they shoulder some of the debt incurred by the various wars. When the colonists objected, the British Parliament levied a Stamp Tax which required that revenue stamps be attached to legal documents, newspapers, playing cards, calendars and other items. In addition, the British imposed a tonnage tax on all vessels entering colonial ports, as well as duties on such products as glass, paper and tea.

Furthermore, the British passed the Quartering Act, forcing the colonists to provide food and shelter for British troops. They also prohibited settlers from moving westward into wilderness areas.

What the British had forgotten, or chosen to disregard, was the basic fact that the quest for liberty and equality had been the motivating force behind the colonization of America for almost 150 years. And from the mixture of the many ethnic and national groups that had survived the hardships of creating a new environment and a new life, emerged an independent, freedom-loving, self-sufficient people; the American. Though many of the colonists felt they still had an allegiance to the mother country, they would no longer accept the role of vassals.

Still Parliament persisted in ignoring the warning signs that were growing more and more ominous. Throughout the colonies, Americans were openly beginning to call for action: Patrick Henry and Thomas Jefferson in Virginia, Samuel Adams in Massachusetts, John Dickinson in Pennsylvania. And acts of violence were becoming more frequent: British troops fired into a taunting mob in Boston; Rhode Islanders burned the British customs schooner *Gaspee* when it ran aground off Providence; a band of 'Indians' boarded British merchantmen in Boston Harbor and threw 15,000 pounds of tea overboard.

In retaliation for the Boston Tea Party, Parliament passed five laws in March, 1774, that the colonists labeled the "Intolerable Acts", four of them specifically designed to punish the people of Massachusetts. The first act ordered the port of Boston closed. The second act stipulated that any British official, military or civilian, charged with a capital offense in the discharge of his duty must be sent to England for trial. The third act revoked the colony's charter, placing it directly under royal control, and prohibited town meetings, except for the purpose of electing officers. The next law revived the Quartering Act, previously repealed, and this time said that occupied buildings might be commandeered. Lastly, the Quebec Act extended the boundary of Quebec southward to the Ohio River, an area in which Virginia, Massachusetts and Connecticut all had claims.

With the implementation of these laws, George III is said to have remarked: "The die is now cast; the colonies must either submit or triumph."

The King soon knew the truth of his forecast. Sufficiently angered by Parliament's edicts to overlook whatever differences they may have had, the colonies made it clear they would not submit. Instead, all but Georgia sent representatives to a meeting at Philadelphia in September, 1774, of the First Continental Congress. There, they resolved (a) to resist the "Intolerable Acts"; (b) to boycott British goods; (c) to send a last-effort, friendly petition to the King in the hopes of having their complaints redressed. Then, they adjourned after pledging to meet again the next May if their rights as Englishmen were still being violated.

No concessions were forthcoming from either the King or Parliament. Instead, on April 18, 1775, Lt General Thomas Gage, commander of the British troops in Boston, sent a detachment to destroy a main supply depot the patriots had cached at Concord, Mass. Paul Revere rode the 16 miles to Lexington, en route to Concord, that night to warn the patriots and give John Hancock and Sam Adams, who were wanted by the British, a chance to escape. The next morning, Captain John Parker and a small band of Minutemen faced the British regulars on the village green at Lexington. "Don't fire unless fired upon," Parker ordered, "but if they mean to have war, let it begin here." That's when the first shot was fired. In the skirmish that followed, eight colonists were killed and 10 wounded. One Redcoat was wounded.

Even with shedding of American blood, not every colonist automatically became a patriot. Some were still loyal to Britain and hoped for an amicable settlement of their differences. But the dream of freedom was too close to fulfillment to be denied. Urged on by the strident voices of John Adams, John Hancock and Patrick Henry, and the persuasive pen of Englishman Thomas Paine in his pamphlet *Common Sense*, the colonists mobilized their forces under George Washington to confront the Redcoats. Then, on July 4, 1776, the Second Continental Congress adopted the Declaration of Independence, and there was no turning back.

During the early years of the Revolution, the American Army, often ill-fed, ill-clothed and ill-housed, seemed on the verge of annihilation, capture or complete disintegration because of desertion, reaching its lowest ebb at its winter encampment at Valley Forge. But, somehow, under Washington's leadership, the army survived, and when it forced General John Burgoyne to surrender his troops at Saratoga in the autumn of 1777, the American cause not only received a boost in morale but also a much-needed commitment from France to aid the colonies.

News of Burgoyne's surrender prompted the British government to send a commission to America to offer the patriots dominion status. King Louis XVI of France, however, signed two treaties that offered the Americans a much better arrangement by recognizing the United States as an independent nation and agreeing to a military alliance.

Incidentally, American naval forces fared better initially than the land forces. The infant United States Navy captured or destroyed about 200 British ships, and American privateers captured about 600 British merchantmen, severely damaging British commerce.

The infusion of French troops and warships put the British on the defensive for the first time. They abandoned full-scale operations in the north and attacked the southern states, particularly South Carolina and Georgia. But the tide of the war was turning in favor of the patriots, and on September 28, 1781, with the French fleet sealing off Chesapeake Bay, American and French troops, commanded by George Washington, surrounded and trapped a British army at Yorktown, Virginia. After a three-week siege, General Charles Cornwallis, the British commander, surrendered his forces and his sword, and Washington informed the Continental Congress that "a Reduction of the British Army...is most happily effected."

When word of Cornwallis' surrender reached England, Lord North, the Prime Minister, was heard to say, despairingly, "Oh God! It's all over", and then he resigned. The new British cabinet determined to start peace negotiations with the Americans as quickly as possible. Though sporadic confrontations between the patriots and British troops continued for more than a year, the Revolution had been won.

The cost in American lives has been estimated to have been as high as 12,000; the cost in dollars, about $104 million. But the impact the war had, in the words of Thomas Paine, "contributed more to enlighten the world, and diffuse a spirit of freedom and liberality among mankind, than any human event...that ever preceded it."

Negotiations for the peace treaty were begun in Paris in April 1782, with Ben Franklin, John Adams, John Jay and Henry Laurens representing the United States. Under the final terms of the treaty that was signed on September 3, 1783, the United States was awarded the rights to all the territory between the Atlantic Coast and the Mississippi River going east to west, and from the Great Lakes and the 49th parallel in the north to the 31st parallel in the south. The Americans were also given the right to fish on the Grand Banks off Newfoundland. On November 25, the last Redcoats left the United States via New York City.

Winning the war was just the first step in the complicated process of establishing the new nation. The second, and equally important one, was the joining together of 13 separate colonies into a cohesive entity, while each wanted to safeguard its autonomy and most were highly distrustful of a strong central government. Fortunately, the infant country was blessed with a bountiful supply of men of conscience, courage and intelligence. On them fell the awesome task of creating a viable framework that would unite the disparate elements without destroying their integrity and also have the resiliency to withstand possible attack both from within and without.

The initial attempt to solve the problem occurred in 1776 when the Second Continental Congress appointed a committee to draw up a plan of union. This plan, known as the *Articles of Confederation*, was adopted by the Congress the following year but required unanimous ratification by the colonies to become law. Twelve states quickly ratified the Articles, but Maryland held out until all the states with claims to western lands ceded them to the United States. That done, Maryland joined the confederation on March 1, 1781, and the Articles went into effect.

It soon became apparent that the constraints placed on Congress by the Articles made the central government almost totally ineffective. On the one hand, Congress could declare war and make peace, establish an army and navy, issue and borrow money, conduct foreign affairs and control Indian affairs. But Congress could not levy taxes or regulate trade either between the states or abroad, and it could not interfere with a state's sovereignty or its citizens.

Each state, regardless of size or population, had one vote in Congress, and the passage of an amendment required the approval of all 13 states.

Perhaps the three most important achievements of the Congress under the Articles were the successful conclusion of the war, the negotiation of the peace treaty, and the adoption of the Northwest Ordinance in 1787.

The ordinance concerned the management of the Northwest Territory, a large unsettled area lying north of the Ohio River, west of Pennsylvania, east of the Mississippi and extending to the northern boundary of the United States. This was the territory that had to be ceded to the United States by the various states before Maryland would ratify the Articles.

Congress, in need of funds, decided to sell land in that area to settlers. Before doing that, however, it adopted an ordinance that set up a plan of government, laid the groundwork for the future social and political climate, and became the model for all territories that later joined the Union as states.

The ordinance postulated three stages through which the territory had to pass before attaining statehood and full self-government. First, Congress appointed a governor, a secretary and three judges. Next, when the adult male population reached 5,000 in the whole territory or any part of it, that area could choose a legislature and send a delegate to Congress who would be permitted to speak but not vote. Then, when the total population got to 60,000, that area could apply for admission into the Union with full equality as a state.

The ordinance banned slavery in the Northwest Territory, guaranteed all persons the rights of trial by jury and freedom of religious worship, and promised fair treatment for the Indians.

Thousands of pioneers responded to the lure of new land and new opportunities, and eventually the territory became five states, and part of a sixth. The five states and their dates of admission to the Union are : Ohio, 1803; Indiana, 1816; Illinois, 1818; Michigan, 1837; Wisconsin, 1848. The sixth state was Minnesota, 1858.

By 1786, the confederation was verging on chaos, with the possibility of it fragmenting into 13 independent countries. Individual states were issuing currency that was so inflated as to be almost worthless. They were raising tariff barriers against each other and refusing to honor their debts. Worst of all, they showed little or no concern for the bigger picture; the problems of sustaining their hard-won republic.

Finally, leaders like George Washington and Alexander Hamilton made it clear that the only way to bring about peace and order and save the country from dissolution was by forming a new national government. To accomplish this task, a constitutional convention was called for May 1787, at Independence Hall, Philadelphia.

Twelve states answered the call, sending 55 delegates to the convention. Only Rhode Island refused to attend because it was fearful that a new constitution might infringe too much on its powers.

Benefiting from the experience of the various colonial governments over the previous 150 years, and guided by the steadying, insightful influences of James Madison, "Father of the Constitution", the delegates hammered out a unique document. It created a system that could function as a strong central government without depriving the people of their basic liberties or the states their rightful responsibilities.

It incorporated a system of checks and balances by giving equal weight to the powers of the executive, legislative and judicial branches. It protected the interests of the large and small states by adopting the compromise suggested by Roger Sherman of Connecticut. This plan called for equal representation in the upper house of the legislature and representation in proportion to population in the lower house.

The convention agreed that instead of requiring unanimous ratification, the Constitution would become the law of the land after only nine states had approved it. With that, the 39 delegates who had remained to the end signed the United States Constitution on September 17, 1787, and sent it out to the states. Delaware became the first state to ratify it (December 7, 1787) and New Hampshire the ninth state (June 21, 1788). Virginia and New York followed.

As specified in the Constitution, the Electoral College, made up of electors selected by the states or their constituents, had the job of electing a Chief Executive from among the eligible cadidates. It unanimously named George Washington as the first President of the country on February 4, 1789, and he was inaugurated on April 30. The first Congress under the new system met in New York City on March 4.

While all this was happening, two states, North Carolina and Rhode Island, refused to ratify the Constitution until they were assured that amendments protecting individual rights would be added to the document as soon as possible. Once they received that assurance, both states joined the Union and sent their representatives to the Federal legislature. The Bill of Rights became law in 1791.

At this time, the United States had a population of about 4,000,000 people, most of whom lived on or near the coast of the Atlantic Ocean. There were perhaps 100,000 pioneers scattered west of the Allegheny Mountains.

Soon after the Constitution was ratified and the government organized and functioning, the country enjoyed a spurt of rapid expansion. Vermont became the 14th state in 1791, followed by Kentucky the next year and Tennessee in 1796. The movement to the west was gaining momentum, and soon after the turn of the century it received an unbelievably fortuitous boost.

THE LOUISIANA PURCHASE

The year was 1801, and Thomas Jefferson had just taken office as the third American President when he learned from the United States minister to England that Spain planned to give part of its colonial territory in America to France. At that time, the Spanish Floridas bordered the United States to the south and westward to the Mississippi, and included New Orleans. Spain's Louisiana Territory started at the Mississippi and blocked the United States to the west.

The key to the problem for the United States was New Orleans, an essential port and collection center for American farmers and merchants in the west who shipped all their surplus produce and products by boat down the rivers, especially the Mississippi, that flowed into the Gulf of Mexico. Fortunately for the Americans, Spain was in a weakened economic and military condition and preferred to do business rather than stir up trouble. In 1795, Spain signed a treaty giving the land-locked Americans the "right of deposit" at New Orleans. This meant that the Americans paid no duty on goods and produce they brought to the city for export, sale to Spanish merchants or storage.

Jefferson knew that this amicable arrangement would be in jeopardy if France, with Napoleon in command, gained control of the Floridas and New Orleans. As it turned out, however, Spain actually ceded its Louisiana Territory to France. Then, a short time after, the Spanish governor of New Orleans suspended the right of deposit for Americans, causing a furor among the westerners.

Meanwhile, American envoys James Monroe and Robert Livingston were trying unsuccessfully to buy the Floridas and New Orleans from Spain or France, whichever would acknowledge ownership at the time, for more than $9 million. But Napoleon was not interested; he had plans for setting up an empire in America. His plans received a serious setback when the army he sent to quell a revolt in Haiti was destroyed. That, plus the impending war with England, made him concerned with the state of his exchequer. So, in a sudden turnabout, Napoleon authorized his finance minister to sell the Louisiana Territory to the Americans. On April 30, 1803, the American envoys, far exceeding their authority, signed an agreement for what has been called "the greatest real estate bargain in history". They bought the Louisiana Territory, including the city of New Orleans for $15 million.

Once the treaty was in hand, the President was faced with a dilemma. The Constitution did not authorize the government to buy foreign land, but it did permit the making of treaties. So, in Jefferson's own words, he "stretched the Constitution until it cracked" and decided that since the acquisition was made by a treaty, it was constitutional.

Jefferson's next problem was to convince Congress to ratify the treaty and to pass a law enabling the government to borrow the purchase money from foreign bankers. In a fervent appeal to Congress, Jefferson said: "Whilst the property and sovereignty of the Mississippi and its waters secure an independent outlet for the produce of the Western states and an uncontrolled navigation through their whole course...the fertility of the country, its climate and extent, promise in due season important aids to our Treasury, as ample provision for our posterity and a wide spread for the blessings of freedom and equal laws."

The treaty was ratified on October 25, 1803. Just what did the United States buy for that $15 million? As a starter, it purchased all the land between the Mississippi River and the Rocky Mountains, stretching from the Gulf of Mexico to the Canadian border. This region, more than 827,000 square miles, doubled the size of the United States, and eventually formed all or parts of 15 states. It gave Americans access to some of the most fertile land and richest mineral deposits in the world. It made possible the growth of the country from ocean to ocean. But, none of this was known until Jefferson sent out the Lewis and Clark expedition in 1804 to explore the area. The party returned two years later, after reaching the Pacific Ocean and traveling about 8,000 miles, and extolled the wonders of the vast domain.

To make this new acquisition more manageable, Congress divided it in two, with one part becoming the Territory of Orleans and the other the District of Louisiana. In 1805, the District was renamed the Territory of Louisiana and seven years later became the Territory of Missouri.

The year 1812 was significant for several other reasons. First, the steamboat *New Orleans* starting at Pittsburgh, Pa., made the initial trip down the Ohio and Mississippi, opening up this major inland waterway for commerce. Then, on April 30, the Territory of Orleans was renamed Louisiana and admitted to the Union as the 18th state with a population of more than 76,000. Shortly thereafter, the Americans and British became engaged in the War of 1812. The last battle took place at New Orleans on January 8, 1815, two weeks after the combatants had signed a peace treaty. General Andrew Jackson and an outnumbered but resolute band of soldiers, frontiersmen and pirates repulsed an invasion by British regulars for the biggest American victory of the war.

THE FLORIDA PURCHASE

The United States' acquisition of Florida eliminated the last foreign colony east of the Mississippi from American soil and completed that section of the country.

From the time of its discovery (1513) by Spanish explorer Juan Ponce de Leon until the United States acquired it (1819), Florida did not play a major role in the settlement of North America. Though the Spaniards had discovered it and named it (Florida means "Feast of Flowers"), the first settlers were French Huguenots, who founded a colony in 1564 on the St Johns River near what is now Jacksonville. Spanish forces, under Don Pedro Menendez de Aviles, drove out the French, treating them as trespassers on land 'owned' by Spain, and established St Augustine in 1565 as the first permanent white settlement on the continent.

The Spaniards had held Florida for 200 years until they sided with the French in the French and Indian War against the English. In the Treaty of Paris (1763), Spain gave Florida to England in exchange for Cuba, which English forces had taken the previous year. The English then divided Florida into East Florida and West Florida, with the latter including part of the land west of Apalachicola River as well as parts of what are now Alabama, Mississippi and Louisiana. East Florida encompassed the remaining area.

Taking advantage of England's involvement in the American Revolution, the Spaniards marched into West Florida and occupied it. In 1781, Britain officially surrendered West Florida to Spain, followed by East Florida two years later. Once the United States gained its independence and began to function as a country, it made numerous offers to buy Florida, but Spain rebuffed them all.

In the early 1800s, Florida became a refuge for runaway slaves and Americans fleeing from the law. It also attracted legitimate settlers, particularly the eastern portion, and in 1812 they tried to establish their independence from Spain but their attempt failed, broken up by Spanish troops.

During the War of 1812, Spain permitted the British navy to use Pensacola as a base, which gave Andrew Jackson enough of a reason to take his troops into Florida and capture Pensacola. After the war, Jackson returned to Florida and defeated the Indians during the First Seminole War (1816-1818). The following year, Spain realized it could not hold on to Florida much longer, so Spain ceded it to the United States in return for the United States paying $5 million in property damages to

American citizens and renouncing any claims to Texas. This became official in 1821, and Congress created the Territory of Florida the next year.

When thousands of settlers moved into this new American territory, they soon began crowding into the land belonging to the Seminoles. In an effort to avoid a conflict, the United States government offered to move the Indians to land in the Oklahoma Territory. Some Indians accepted, but those who refused to leave their homes soon found the situation to be intolerable. Finally, in despair and frustration, the Indians started the Second Seminole War in 1835 by attacking a detachment of Federal troops. The war lasted until 1842, by which time the Indians were virtually wiped out. Most of the survivors moved away, leaving a small band behind. Though the fighting had stopped, the Seminoles remained at war with the United States until 1934 when they signed a peace treaty.

Florida was admitted to the Union as the 27th state in 1845. It had a population of over 66,000 and was designated a slave state even though most of its farmers did not own slaves and worked their small farms themselves.

THE TEXAS ANNEXATION

The next major land area to become part of the United States was the region to the south and west of the Louisiana Purchase called Texas. This was the area to which the United States had given up all claims when Spain ceded Florida in the 1819 treaty.

The modern history of Texas goes back to the early sixteenth century when Spanish adventurers prowled the New World in search of "gold, glory and God". The Spaniard usually credited with being the first white man to set foot on Texas soil was Alonzo Alvarez de Pineda, who had been commissioned to map the coastline of the Gulf of Mexico from Florida to Mexico; the year: 1519.

He was followed by Alvar Nunez Cabeza de Vaca, whose expedition was shipwrecked on the Texas coast. He and three companions spent eight years wandering among various Indian tribes before reaching a Spanish settlement in Mexico. There, they told stories of cities of great wealth (the Seven Cities of Cibola) so convincingly that the Spaniards invested much time, money and manpower in numerous expeditions to find these fabled places, all to no avail.

The French set up a settlement and joined the hunt in 1685 when Robert Cavelier, Sieur de la Salle, landed at Matagorda Bay. After establishing Fort Saint Louis, La Salle explored the area for gold and silver and was killed by one of his own men. Indians then destroyed the fort.

Spain's major accomplishment in Texas was the founding of a string of missions throughout the area, starting with two in 1682 near present-day El Paso. In 1772, San Antonio became the seat of the Spanish Government for that region. But few Spaniards were interested in colonizing the area, and by 1793, there were only about 7,000 white settlers in residence in all of Texas.

In 1821, Mexico broke away from Spain and included Texas in the newly-declared Empire of Mexico. Three years later, Mexico became a republic.

No one realized it then, but the financial problems of one man were about to set in motion a series of events that would change the course of Texas history, and the map of the United States. Moses Austin, born a Connecticut Yankee, had been a banker in the Spanish-held territory of Missouri for 20 years until he was ruined by a financial panic in 1819. In an effort to recoup his losses, Austin applied for and received from the Mexican government a charter granting lands for colonization in Texas to 200 families.

When Austin died before he could implement his plan to found a new colony, the charter was transferred to his son, Stephen. Under the terms of the charter, the American colonists would receive land tax free for seven years if they complied with two prerequisites. The first stipulation was that they become Mexican citizens; the second, all colonists had to be or become practicing Catholics.

In 1821-22, Stephen Austin moved the first families to settlements at Washington-on-the-Brazos and Columbus in southeast Texas. The following year he founded San Felipe de Austin in what is now Austin County. Other American colonizers, whom the Mexicans called *empresarios*, soon emulated Austin, and by 1827 there were more than 12,000 American settlers in Texas. Many of them were Southern cotton growers who had brought their slaves with them.

This unexpectedly large influx of Americans began to alarm the Mexican government and created friction between the Mexicans and the independent-minded colonists. To slow the flood of American immigrants and also to reinforce their own authority, Mexican officials made some radical changes when the seven-year grace period in the grants expired. They abolished slavery in Texas and banned the importation of slaves. They restricted immigration to proven Catholics, not converts who made empty promises to embrace the Church. Then, they levied heavy taxes on the nonconformers.

When these restrictions failed to stem the tide, the Mexicans closed down all American immigration to Texas in 1830. By now, the colonists and the Mexicans were both working on very short fuses. The resentment of the Americans was further exacerbated when, in 1834, General Antonio Lopez de Santa Anna overthrew the constitutional government of Mexico and seized power. As part of his solution for dealing with the recalcitrant Americans, he attached Texas to the Mexican state of Coahuila, thereby reducing its status and importance and placing another layer of bureaucracy between the colonists and the Mexican government. Santa Anna also tried to force the settlers to buy only Mexican products from Mexican merchants by imposing excessive duties on imports.

To the colonists whose heritage was formed on a foundation of liberty and independence, there was only one appropriate solution to their dilemma; revolt against the oppressive authority.

In 1835, Americans in Texas took up arms, and, after several small actions against Mexican troops, their leaders met at San Felipe de Austin and organized a temporary government. Then, they marched on San Antonio and took the city on December 11. There, the rebellious Texans declared their independence from

Mexico and elected a rugged frontiersman and ex-soldier, Sam Houston, as commander-in-chief of the armies of the Republic of Texas.

In reality, these armies were little more than scattered bands of Texans, numbering fewer than 1,000 men all told. But, they had the incredible conceit to believe they could win no matter how the odds were stacked against them. This attitude also carried over into a disdain for taking orders from any authority, which led to the annihilation of one of these small bands, and the creation of a national memorial.

Santa Anna could not allow the loss of San Antonio to go unchallenged, so he crossed the Rio Grande River with 7,000 troops and marched on the city. The Texans refused to heed Houston's orders to retreat, and, instead, barricaded themselves in an old Spanish mission called the Alamo. After an 11-day siege, the Alamo fell to Santa Anna on March 6, 1836, and every one of its 188 defenders was killed.

Hoping to put down the revolution quickly, Santa Anna chased after Sam Houston and his dwindling army, trying to corner them for a showdown battle. Along the way, the Mexican general ordered more than 300 Texan prisoners shot to death at a town called Goliad. Then, on April 20, when Santa Anna arrived at a ferry crossing at the San Jacinto River (near present-day Houston), he found Houston waiting for him. With his forces outnumbering the Texans almost two to one, his troops weary from the chase, and not believing that Houston would dare to attack him, Santa Anna rested his army.

Houston did attack, however, catching half the enemy troops asleep. To the cries of "Remember the Alamo" and "Remember Goliad", the Texans swarmed over the enemy, killing or capturing all 1,450 Mexicans and taking Santa Anna prisoner. The Texans lost 16 killed and 24 wounded out of an army of under 800. That victory ended the war and ensured the independence of Texas.

Once free of Mexican domination, Texas became a republic, and in its first national election the voters chose Sam Houston as President. They also voted to join the Union, but it would be almost ten years before that actually happened.

Andrew Jackson, then serving out his second term as President of the United States, wanted very much to have Texas become a state during his administration but refrained from pressing the point. At that time, slavery had begun to be an inflammatory issue, with the country equally divided between slave and free states. The admission of Texas as a slave state would have upset that balance and created problems that no one wanted to face at that time.

It was not until the last days of President Tyler's administration that both houses of Congress passed a joint resolution to admit Texas as a state, the only time such a procedure was used. The reason: statehood for Texas was still a volatile issue, and the joint resolution required fewer votes of approval than an act of Congress.

The terms of the statehood agreement allowed Texas to keep its public lands, but it had to pay its own public debts. The agreement gave the Federal government the authority to settle all boundary disputes with other countries, a proviso that would soon be useful to the expansionist interests of the United States. It also stated that at some later date, Texas could split itself into as many as four more states.

President Tyler signed the resolution on March 1, 1845, three days before leaving the White House to his successor James K. Polk. On December 29 of that year, Texas officially became the 28th state in the Union and sent Sam Houston to the United States Senate.

THE OREGON REGION

Americans knew very little about the northwest part of North America called Oregon until the Lewis and Clark expedition returned in 1806 after a two-year journey. Lewis and Clark reached the mouth of the Columbia River and then the Pacific Ocean. But even though they covered thousands of miles by land (and returned with glowing reports) they had not seen even half of the Oregon region, an area that extended from the northern border of Spanish-owned California to the southern boundary of Alaska, which was claimed by Russia. In width, it reached from the Rocky mountains westward to the Pacific.

Some historians say that Spanish sailors in the late 1500s may have been the first white men to see the Oregon coast, and that Sir Francis Drake may have touched southern Oregon in 1579. But it was another 200 years (1778) before sea captain James Cook of England discovered and named Cape Foulweather, north of Yaquina Bay, and still another decade before an American (Robert Gray) landed on the Oregon coast. In 1792, Gray discovered the Columbia River, which he named after his ship, and George Vancouver of Great Britain mapped the coast.

Because there was no clear-cut claimant to the region, a very awkward situation developed. Four countries, the United States, Great Britain, Spain and Russia, claimed parts of it. The problem was partially solved when in 1819 Spain relinquished its claim north of the 42nd parallel, which was California's northern border. Russia later yielded its interests below the 54th parallel, Alaska's southern boundary. Meanwhile, Great Britain and the United States worked out an accommodation in 1818 that permitted settlers from both countries to trade and colonize in the area. They renewed that agreement in 1827.

Up to this time, the only white men who had shown any strong interest in living there were the fur trappers, those legendary loners known as the Mountain Men. The first settlement in the area was a fur trading post on the Columbia River named Astoria. It was founded in 1811 by the Pacific Fur Company, owned by John Jacob Astor of New York.

Fourteen years later, the Hudson's Bay Company of England set up a rival trading post nearby called Fort Vancouver. The man in charge of operations there for 20 years, John McLoughlin, later became an American citizen, and is honored today as the "Father of Oregon".

Then, some Methodist missionaries started a settlement in the Willamette Valley, and word began filtering eastward about the richness and fertility of the land. That kind of news, plus a depression in 1837 that had wiped out many farmers, and the urging of an expansionist group in Congress for Americans to follow their "manifest destiny" to the Pacific, combined to start a migration to Oregon.

In 1841, settlers had begun to make the trek over the Oregon Trail – 2,000 miles of some of the roughest terrain in the country. From Independence, Missouri, where the wagon trains made up, to the Willamette Valley took six months of slow traveling through prairies and deserts, across mountains and flooded rivers. In addition, those pioneer families had to survive Indian attacks and disease, shortages of food and water, and capricious weather. But enough of them made it to encourage others, and in 1843, an estimated 1,000 people traveled the Oregon Trail. Two years later, the number jumped to 3,000 men, women and children.

The flood of Americans into Oregon took the British by surprise, and they suddenly became fearful of losing out in that area. They wanted to settle the boundary dispute and offered to set the line at the Columbia River, but the Americans felt confident they could get the whole region right up to Alaska. In fact, James K. Polk, a little-known Democratic candidate used "Fifty Four Forty or Fight" as a slogan in his winning Presidential campaign. The slogan referred to Alaska's southern border at the 54th parallel.

A possible conflict was avoided when Polk wisely decided to forego his campaign promise. The United States and Britain worked out a compromise in 1846 that divided the disputed region at the 49th parallel from the Rockies to the Pacific. Britain received the upper portion, and the United States the lower part. Now, for the first time, the east/west borders of the United States reached from coast to coast.

Congress designated Oregon as a territory in 1848, and its present boundaries were set in 1853 when Congress divided the area, making the upper half into the Washington Territory.

When the great migration slowed to a trickle, Congress tried to spur territorial development through a unique measure called the Donation Land Law of 1850. This law offered 320 acres of land to any male American citizen over 18 who settled in Oregon and cultivated his claim for four years. If married, his wife was eligible for the same grant. The offer was valid only until December, 1850. After that date and until December, 1855, the recipient had to be at least 21 years old and his grant would be for only 160 acres.

On February 14, 1859, Oregon became the 33rd state to join the Union. It had a population then of more than 52,000.

THE MEXICAN CESSION

With Texas safely in the Union, and the dispute with Britain over the boundary of the Oregon Territory settled, the expansionists in America set their sights on California, a province of the Republic of Mexico.

Mexico's claim to California dated back 300 years to 1542, the year that Juan Rodriguez Cabrillo, a Portuguese sea captain employed by Spain, sailed from New Spain (Mexico) to search for golden cities to loot and a west-to-east waterway linking the Pacific and Atlantic oceans. Cabrillo is credited with being the first European to see the coast of California, stopping at San Diego Bay before venturing further north.

England also had an early claim on California because of Sir Francis Drake, who touched the California coast in 1579 during his famous globe-girdling voyage, and named the area New Albion. But, it was the Spaniards, and later the Mexicans, who established missions, then presidios (military forts) and finally pueblos (villages).

The first American vessel to arrive, the *Otter*, did not reach California until 1796, opening the way for others to make trading trips. The only Americans to come by land were the Mountain Men who trapped up and down the Pacific coast, regardless of who owned the territory. In 1841, the first wagon train of American settlers blazed a trail to California, and it was followed soon after by many others. Then, to the consternation of Mexican authorities, John Charles Fremont led a party of military surveyors into California in 1844.

When Fremont returned in March, 1846, the Mexicans, already disturbed by the incursion of American settlers, and fearful of the intentions of the surveying group, ordered his party to leave the province. In defiance of the order, Fremont encamped his detachment about 25 miles from Monterey, raised the American flag and started to build a small fort. He then reconsidered his position and left the area one night. Six weeks later, Mexico and the United States were at war.

Diplomatic relations between the two countries had been getting progressively more strained ever since Texas won its independence. Mexico had refused to recognize Texas as a republic and was resentful, though helpless to do anything about it, when the United States welcomed the new nation. The Mexican government then warned the United States that it would declare war if Texas gained admittance to the Union. When Texas did become a state in 1845, Mexico broke off diplomatic relations with the United States.

At another time, and without the fever of manifest destiny and frontierism that was surging through America, calmer heads would have prevailed and settled matters by peaceful means rather than war. Mexico, already undergoing internal difficulties, was virtually in a state of revolution and would have been content with a face-saving gesture. There were two issues, however, that became the basis for the ensuing conflict.

First, there was a boundary dispute between Texas and Mexico, with the former claiming the Rio Grande as its western border and the latter saying that Texas extended only as far as the Nueces River. The second issue concerned $3,000,000 in compensation to American citizens for losses they sustained in Mexico through revolution, theft and confiscation since the 1820s.

President James Polk, an ardent expansionist, sent his envoy, John Slidell, to Mexico City with an offer of $25 million and the cancellation of all claims for damages in return for setting the Rio Grande as the boundary for Texas plus the cession of New Mexico and California to the United States. If Mexico refused to part with New Mexico and California, Slidell's next offer was to cancel all claims in exchange for the Rio Grande boundary.

Unfortunately, the political situation in Mexico City was so unstable that no high-level official would see Slidell. He returned to Washington and recommended that the Mexicans be "chastised".

In March, 1846, President Polk ordered an army of 3,000, commanded by Major General Zachary Taylor, to move from its position on the Nueces to the Rio Grande. The Americans were in place on the Rio Grande, overlooking Matamoros, the principal Mexican city in the area, by mid-April. Then, on April 25, a Mexican detachment crossed the river and ambushed a small scouting party of U.S. Cavalry.

When the news that 15 U.S. soldiers had been killed reached Washington, D.C., President Polk called Congress into session and announced that Mexican troops had invaded United States territory and "shed American blood upon American soil", ignoring the fact that the ownership of the area was still unclear. Congress responded by declaring war on Mexico and appropriating $10 million to fund the recruitment of 50,000 volunteers.

With Zach Taylor's army crushing all resistance in north and central Mexico, and General Winfield Scott launching his campaign in the south with the first successful amphibious landing of American troops on foreign soil (at Vera Cruz), the Mexicans found themselves fighting a losing war on all fronts. Mexico City fell to the invaders 16 months after the American Congress had declared war. The conflict was over.

At the same time that Taylor had led his troops south of the Rio Grande, General Stephen Kearny left Fort Leavenworth with 1,700 troops and occupied Santa Fe, New Mexico. Then, sending part of his army across the Rio Grande to seize Chihuahua, Kearny led the rest of it across the desert to California. He arrived just in time for the final collapse of Mexican resistance there which had been under attack from sea and land units commanded by Naval Captain Robert Stockton and Army Captain John Fremont.

On February 2, 1848, American and Mexican negotiators met at the little village of Guadalupe Hidalgo and signed a peace treaty that gave the United States everything that President Polk had originally wanted. Mexico yielded the disputed area between the Nueces and Rio Grande Rivers, and the territories of New Mexico and California. In return, the United States paid Mexico $15 million for the territories.

The Mexican War, though considered minor in terms of time, men, material and money expended, nevertheless had major consequences for the United States. The new territories added 525,000 square miles to this country, putting in place the penultimate piece in the continental mosaic that gave the United States dominion from coast to coast. It also precluded any further attempt by foreign powers at colonization here.

The acquisition of New Mexico and California brought on bitter arguments between the North and South over whether the territories would become slave or free states. Only Henry Clay's Compromise of 1850 temporarily appeased advocates of the pro- and anti-slavery factions and prevented a split in the Union for another decade. Under the terms of the Compromise, California was admitted to the Union in 1850 as a free state. It became the 31st state.

Lastly, the Mexican War served as a training ground for many officers who would later fight in the Civil War. Among them were Ulysses S. Grant, Robert E. Lee, William T. Sherman, Jefferson Davis, Thomas "Stonewall" Jackson, George Meade and George McClellan.

THE GADSDEN PURCHASE

The last parcel of real estate needed to complete the continental boundaries of the United States as they are today was acquired in an outright purchase from Mexico in a treaty signed on December 30, 1853.

The Treaty of Guadalupe Hidalgo ending the Mexican War did not adequately define the westernmost border between the two countries. The area in question was a strip of land south of the Gila River in what later became the states of Arizona and New Mexico.

James Gadsden, a railroad executive serving as the United States Minister to Mexico, wanted to clear up the boundary question, but he also saw that the extra land would give the United States a good southern railroad route to the Pacific Coast. He pressed the negotiations with Mexican president Santa Anna (the same man who had wiped out the Alamo defenders) and bought 29,640 square miles for $10 million. With the Gadsden Purchase, the boundaries for the contiguous 48 states were finally in place.

THE ALASKA PURCHASE

America's next best real estate bargain, after the Louisiana Purchase, was the Alaska Purchase although critics at the time derided it as "Seward's Folly", and "Seward's Icebox".

On March 30, 1867, William Seward, then United States Secretary of State, agreed to buy the Russian territory of Alaska for $7,200,000, which amounted to about two cents an acre. This gave the United States an area covering 591,004 square miles, stretching 2,200 miles from east to west, 1,200 miles from north to south, with 6,600 miles of coastline.

More than twice the size of Texas and almost one-fifth as large as the rest of the United States, Alaska is closer to Russia than it is to the lower 48. Only 51 miles separate the Alaskan mainland from the U.S.S.R., while 500 miles of Canada separate it from the state of Washington. About one-third of Alaska lies north of the Arctic Circle, but its northernmost boundary is still 1,300 miles south of the North Pole.

The original inhabitants of Alaska were Eskimos, Aleuts, who were related to the Eskimos, and Indians. It was not until 1741 that the first outsider, Vitus Bering, a Danish sea captain commissioned by Czar Peter the Great of Russia to explore the North Pacific, landed on Kayak Island off the coast of southeastern Alaska. More than 40 years later, the first white settlement, a trading post for trappers and traders, was established on Kodiak Island.

Then, in 1799, the Russian-American Company, chartered by Russia to conduct trade in Alaska, set up shop at Sitka and became the only law and government in the territory for the next 68 years. During most of that time, the Russians used the Indians and Aleuts as virtual slave labor while they decimated the population of fur-bearing animals. During the 1820s, the Russians agreed with the United States and Britain to setting the 54th parallel as the southern boundary of their territory in America. They also granted both countries the privilege of trading along the Alaskan coast.

In the 1850s, the Russian trading company had just about phased out its business, forcing the Russian government to get involved. But after the Russian military losses in the Crimean War (1853-56), the government was anxious to make a deal for Alaska and so was William Seward.

For its first 17 years under the American flag, Alaska was treated with great indifference. It had no government but was passed from one Federal department to another, first War, then Treasury, and then Navy.

As settlers began to drift into the territory and the first salmon canneries were built to take advantage of Alaska's rich fisheries, Congress passed the first Organic Act in 1884. This legislation made Alaska a "civil and judicial district" with a code of laws and a Federal court, but the power to enact laws remained with Congress.

Alaska was flooded with newcomers when gold was discovered in the Klondike region of the Yukon Territory in 1896. Towns like Skagway sprang up overnight and prospered as the traffic flowed through them en route to the Klondike. Alaska's population took another jump when other gold strikes were made in Nome and Fairbanks. Meanwhile, more canneries were built along the coast, and copper was found in the south-central part of the area.

A sure sign that Alaska was rapidly maturing occurred in 1906, when the residents elected their first delegate to Congress. He was permitted to address the House of Representatives but had no vote. The next step happened in 1912 when Congress passed the second Organic Act, which made Alaska officially a U.S. territory and authorized the creation of a legislature with limited powers.

It took World War II to make the Federal government realize the military importance of Alaska because of its closeness to Asia. Many military installations were quickly built and manned by thousands of American troops. The government built the Alaska Highway just so it could keep these bases supplied. That did not stop the Japanese, however. They bombed Dutch Harbor in the Aleutians and occupied three of the islands, Agattu, Attu and Kiska, the only parts of North America ever invaded by the enemy. American troops regained the islands early in 1943.

After campaigning for statehood for many years and adopting a constitution in 1956 (to go into effect when admitted), Alaskans finally had reason to celebrate on June 30, 1958, when Congress voted to admit them to the Union. On January 3, 1959, a Presidential proclamation by Dwight D. Eisenhower made Alaska the 49th state.

THE ANNEXATION OF HAWAII

Hawaii, the newest star in Old Glory's field of blue, has undoubtedly the most unusual physical and ethnic characteristics of any state in the Union.

It is the only state that is not on the mainland of North America. It consists of a 1,610-mile-long chain of 132 islands in the middle of the Pacific Ocean, more than 2,400 miles west of the American Pacific Coast. It is further south than any mainland southern state, with its capital city, Honolulu, on a parallel with central Mexico. There are eight principal islands, which lie at the southeastern end of the chain, and of the eight, Oahu is the most important, having the highest concentration of people and the capital city.

The only state that was once an independent monarchy, Hawaii today is one of the world's great "melting pots", with a polyglot population made up of people of Polynesian, Chinese, Filipino and Japanese descent, plus Americans of various ethnic origins and other Caucasian groups. And each of these peoples has contributed something to the customs, culture and lifestyle of the islands.

The history of Hawaii dates back more than 2,000 years, when, according to island legend, the first Polynesians arrived in large canoes. A second wave of Polynesians, presumably from Tahiti, is said to have reached the islands about 1200 A.D. It is thought that some time in the 16th century, sea captains from Europe or the Orient may have stopped there, but the first confirmed landing occurred on January 18, 1778. On that date, British Navy Captain James Cook, on an exploratory expedition in the Pacific, discovered the Hawaiian Islands. Cook spent two weeks exploring the islands and trading with the islanders, and then left after naming the area the Sandwich Islands, in honor of The First Lord of the British Admiralty, the Earl of Sandwich.

Cook returned to Hawaii in November and was killed in early 1779 during a fight between his men and natives. But his discovery had a profound effect on the future of the islands, opening them up to other explorers and traders, who not only introduced new products to the Hawaiians but also new diseases that proved to be deadly for them.

At the time of Cook's visits, the islands were ruled individually by local chiefs. By 1795, however, the main islands, except for Kauai and Niihau, had been united by King Kamehameha I. The two holdouts accepted his rule in 1810. Nine years later, Kamehameha II abolished the Hawaiian religion that practiced human sacrifice, idol worship and belief in many gods, an act that could be considered providential because within 12 months the brig *Thaddeus* dropped anchor at Hawaii and disembarked a group of Protestant missionaries. Within a relatively short time, the missionaries had converted most of the islanders to Christianity.

Initially, the major sources of income for the islands came from providing merchantmen and whalers with fresh water and supplies, and exporting sandalwood to China. Although there is a record of pineapple plants being imported as early as 1813 (they are not indigenous to Hawaii), commercial production did not begin until late in the century when 1,000 plants were brought in from the island of Jamaica. The first permanent sugar plantation was started on Kauai in 1835 by an American company.

The growth of agricultural production coupled with a depletion of the local labor force, due primarily to disease, led to the importation of laborers from other countries and the onset of Hawaii's multinational population. First came the Chinese, then the new Polynesians and the Japanese, followed by the Portuguese, Filipinos, Koreans and Puerto Ricans.

In 1840, the government of Hawaii changed from a somewhat benevolent autocracy to a constitutional monarchy when the islands adopted a constitution that called for a legislature and a supreme court. The legislature was comprised of a council of chiefs and an elected house of representatives. With that change, the Kingdom of Hawaii was recognized as an independent government by the United States, Great Britain and France.

The monarchy remained intact until 1893 when a bloodless revolution toppled Queen Liliuokalani, who had succeeded to the throne two years earlier. The Queen foolishly tried to increase her power beyond her constitutional authority and provoked a rebellious reaction, led by a small group of Americans, Englishmen and Germans. The Queen was deposed and the revolutionaries formed the Republic of Hawaii and made Judge Sanford B. Dole the first and only president of the republic.

The government of the republic continued until a powerful lobby of American planters and businessmen, wanting to get under the protective umbrella of U.S. military might and also gain some important tax advantages, persuaded the United States to annex Hawaii. They achieved their purpose of August 12, 1898, and two years later the Hawaiian Islands were made U.S. territory. Sanford Dole was then appointed the first governor.

Recognizing the strategic value of the islands, the U.S. Navy started construction of the Pearl Harbor Naval Base just before the outbreak of World War I. The U.S. Army, in turn, also built bases around Honolulu. However, Hawaii ws not threatened until December 7, 1941, when planes of the Japanese Navy attacked Pearl Harbor and the airfield of Oahu. The United States was plunged into World War II on the side of the Allies against the Axis powers.

Following the war, President Harry Truman recommended that Hawaii be admitted to the Union. Encouraged by his backing, Hawaiians drew up and approved a constitution to become effective when they received statehood, but that long-awaited event did not happen until March 11, 1959. From 1903 until that date in 1959, a total of 59 bills concerning statehood for Hawaii had been presented to Congress before the senate finally approved one. The House passed it the next day, and President Eisenhower signed it on March 18. The Hawaiian citizenry overwhelmingly voted in favor of statehood in June, and on August 21, Hawaii became the 50th state.

THE UNITED STATES AT LARGE

No recounting of the growth and development of the United States would be complete without some acknowledgement of the outlying regions that fly the Stars and Stripes. Here are some of the more important ones.

Puerto Rico (a Commonwealth)
Discovered by Columbus in 1493 on his second voyage and claimed for Spain, Puerto Rico is probably the only part of the United States where he actually landed. This verdant island, whose Spanish name translates to "Rich Port" in English, lies a little more that 1,000 miles southeast of the tip of Florida and forms a section of the barrier between the Atlantic Ocean and the Caribbean Sea.

Though it has been a part of the United States since 1898 when Spain relinquished it after the Spanish-American War, Puerto Rico's principal language and customs still reflect its Spanish heritage. The first colony was founded by Juan Ponce de Leon in 1508, and it grew despite suffering from hurricanes and disease as well as withstanding attacks by Indians, the Dutch, the English and the French.

In 1917, Congress gave American citizenship to the Puerto Ricans, and they reciprocated by flocking to join the armed forces in World War I, and in every subsequent conflict. The first island-born governor was appointed in 1946 by President Truman, and one year later Congress granted the islanders the right to elect their own governor.

Public Law 600, authorizing Puerto Rico to write its own constitution, passed Congress in 1950. That document received Congressional approval on July 1, 1952, and on July 25, Puerto Rico became a self-governing commonwealth.

Guam (a Territory)
On August 1, 1950, Guam became a U.S. territory and its people American citizens. The U.S. Department of the Interior is responsible for the supervision of Guam, but the governor and lieutenant governor are elected and a non-voting delegate is sent to the U.S. House. Local laws are enacted by an elective unicameral legislature.

This Pacific island, located at the south end of the Mariana group that includes Rota, Saipan and Tinian, is part of a submerged volcanic mountain range that runs northward towards Japan for 1,565 miles. Guam is about 30 miles long, varies from four to 10 miles in width and lies 1,500 miles east of the Philippines.

Discovered, along with Rota, by the Portuguese navigator Ferdinand Magellan in 1521, he called both of them the Islas de los Ladrones (Islands of Thieves) because the natives were so adept at stealing things from his ship. Spain made Guam a possession in 1561, but it was not until 100 years later, after the arrival of Spanish Jesuits, that Spain appointed its own government there. Guam remained under Spanish control until 1898, when it was ceded to the United States under the terms of the Treaty of Paris at the end of the Spanish-American War. Spain then sold the other islands in the chain to Germany.

The other islands in the Mariana chain are governed by

the United States as part of the United Nations Trust Territory of the Pacific Islands. They are now moving towards independence.

The Virgin Islands (a Territory)
About 40 miles east of Puerto Rico, between the Atlantic Ocean and the Caribbean Sea, lie St Croix, St John and St Thomas, the Virgin Islands of the United States. They form the western end of the West Indian island chain called the Lesser Antilles. Immediately to the east, and also part of the chain, are the British Virgin Islands.

Discovered by Columbus during his 1493 voyage, he gave the island group the name Virgin Islands in honor of St Ursula and her 11,000 maiden companions who had been martyred by the Huns. Although Columbus claimed all the islands for Spain, the Spaniards never settled on them, but used them as places to hide their treasure ships from pirates.

It is thought that the English settlers who were on their way to found Jamestown, Va., may have stopped at the islands, but no permanent settlement was established until 1625 when the English and Dutch landed on St Croix. Then the Danes claimed St Thomas in 1666, and, after one failure succeeded in setting up a permanent colony six years later. The Danes also settled on St John.

St Croix subsequently underwent several changes of ownership in a short time span. First, the Spaniards from Puerto Rico drove out the English and Dutch, and they were driven out by the French, who sold St Croix to the Danes in 1733 for $150,000. After trying unsuccessfully for approximately 200 years to develop the islands commercially, Denmark sold them to the United States for $25,000,000. The transfer became effective on March 31, 1917.

Virgin Islanders became American citizens in 1927, and, if they could read and write English, were later granted the right to vote in local elections but not in national elections.

The Virgin Islands have the status of a territory and are administered by the U.S. Department of the Interior. Voters have been electing their own governor since 1970. The islands' legislature is a unicameral body of senators who are elected to two-year terms. A non-voting delegate has been sent to the U.S. House since 1972. At this time, the islands do not have their own constitution, having rejected the most recent draft in 1981. The Revised Organic Act of the Virgin Islands, which Congress passed in 1954, still serves that function.

The principal industry of the islands is tourism, followed by oil refining, bauxite processing and rum.

American Samoa (a Territory)
American Samoa is part of a 14-island volcanic chain that is spread over an area of about 1,170 square miles in the South Pacific. The Islands are divided by the 171st meridian of west longitude, with those west of the line forming Western Samoa, a free and independent country since 1962. East of the line is American Samoa, which lies 4,800 miles southwest of San Francisco and has a total land mass of 76 square miles. Tutuila, the largest and most important island in the American sector, takes up 54 square miles and has the only good harbor in Samoa, the port of Pago Pago. Native

inhabitants of Samoa are U.S. nationals but not American citizens.

The U.S. Navy has had a base on Tutuila since 1872, but it was an 1889 treaty with Great Britain and Germany that gave the United States control of the islands east of the meridian. Germany controlled the islands west of the line until the League of Nations awarded them to New Zealand in 1920.

American Samoa held its first popular election for governor in 1977. The next year, Congress gave the islands a non-voting delegate in the House. Under the constitution it adopted in 1960, Samoa has its own local legislature. In addition, there is an Inter-Samoa Consultative Committee, composed of members from both Samoas, to resolve problems of mutual concern.

Wake Island (a Possession)
In the west-central Pacific Ocean, 2,300 miles west of Honolulu and almost 2,000 miles southeast of Tokyo, is a tiny atoll called Wake Island. Discovered by the British in 1796, and surveyed many years later by a U.S. Navy expedition, the once-uninhabited, triangular-shaped atoll is comprised of three tiny islets and a reef-enclosed shallow lagoon. The entire land mass covers about three square miles.

Wake was captured by the Japanese in December, 1941, after a stubborn defense by a small military and civilian garrison, and was returned to the United States at the end of the war. It is administered today by the U.S. Air Force.

Midway Island (a Possession)
Another speck in the Pacific, Midway is an atoll made up of two islands that have a combined land area of two square miles. It is located 1,300 miles northwest of Honolulu.

Midway was discovered by the United States in 1859 and annexed in 1867. It initially served as a cable relay station, and an airport was added in the 1930s.

From June 4 to June 6, 1942, the sea around Midway became the arena for the first decisive U.S. naval victory over the Japanese. Some military experts believe that the Battle of Midway was the turning point in the Pacific War.

Midway today is controlled by the U.S. Navy Department.

Panama Canal Zone
A pact in 1903 between the United States and the recently-independent Republic of Panama marked the beginning of one of man's greatest engineering feats – the building of the Panama Canal. By agreement, Panama allocated a strip of land 10 miles wide and extending 40 miles between the Atlantic and Pacific Oceans to be called the Canal Zone, through which the Canal would run.

The United States was given the right to build and operate the Canal and to govern the Zone in return for paying Panama an annual guaranteed rental. Panama retained its authority over the cities of Colon and Panama which were located at either end of the Canal. The basic agreements were changed in 1979, and Panama took over the land, dry docks, ports and railroads in the Zone. Full control of the Canal will revert to Panama in the year 2000.

THE UNITED STATES TODAY

As the 20th century winds down and the United States is well into its third century as a member of the family of nations, it is probably safe to predict that the Union will survive. From the time of its birth until now, it has withstood the test of financial panic, economic depression, a civil war that temporarily divided it, two World Wars and other military involvements, even corruption and malfeasance in high places. Out of these trials and tribulations has emerged one of the world's superpowers.

Beginning with two tiny settlements in the early 17th century, Jamestown in the south and Plymouth in the north, the United States now occupies 3,623,420 square miles, making it the fourth largest country in the world behind the U.S.S.R., Canada and mainland China. And from those first disparate but intrepid little bands of colonists, and the subsequent waves of ethnic and racial groups that followed, this nation of immigrants has produced a population of approximately 229 million which ranks fourth in the world after mainland China, India and the U.S.S.R.

Racially, the population of America is a little more than 83 percent white, almost 12 percent black, with other races making up the remaining percentage. Religiously, the country is about 65 percent Protestant, 25 percent Roman Catholic, 3 percent Jewish, and the rest of other or no affiliation. Life expectancy for the total population is 74 years, an increase of 15 years over the 1930 census figure of 59 years. Per capita income is $11,596.

America is an extremely mobile country, with 3,918,000 miles of paved roads to accommodate 159,029,000 motor vehicles, of which 123,467,000 are passenger cars. It has four of the five busiest airports in the world in terms of total annual passenger traffic. Chicago's O'Hare leads the way followed by Atlanta International, Los Angeles International, London's Heathrow, and New York's John F. Kennedy.

The United States has not only grown outward, it has also grown upward and now boasts the world's five tallest buildings. They are, in descending order, the Sears Tower (Chicago), the World Trade Center (New York), the Empire State Building (New York), the Standard Oil of Indiana Building, and the John Hancock Building (Chicago).

But what is America really like? To know America is to know something about the sections that have been joined together over the past 200 years to make the big picture.

The New England States
New England, an area of 66,600 square miles, is bordered by Canada on the north, the Atlantic Ocean on the east, Long Island Sound on the south, and New York State on the west. Within these boundaries lie six states: Massachusetts, Connecticut, Rhode Island, Vermont, New Hampshire and Maine.

The topographical features of the region, consisting of a low coastal plain, several mountain ranges and fertile river valleys, and two rock-strewn uplands, run north and south, thereby depriving New England of a natural land or water route to the West. This phenomenon had the salutary effect of making New England the most unified region in the country in terms of geography, history and culture. It prevented settlers from moving westward, dispersing and losing touch with their common heritage. Instead, as the colonists branched out from the original Massachusetts settlements, they had to follow the north-south line, which made for easier communication, closer contact, and a natural extension of their culture.

Named by Captain John Smith of Jamestown fame, who explored the area in 1614, New England is a region whose rugged terrain and long, often bitter winters might have defeated less determined colonists than the Pilgrims and the Puritans. But they had risked all to make the hazardous voyage to the New World, and no obstacle of man or nature was going to deny them the opportunity to start a new life according to their own dictates. The same qualities and values have pervaded New England life ever since.

Usually of a more conservative bent, New Englanders were among the earliest and most ardent advocates of independence from Great Britain. And it was they who brought the issue to a head with the Boston Tea Party, the first armed confrontation with British troops at Lexington and Concord, and the Battle of Bunker Hill.

Aside from their dedication to the pursuit of independence and liberty, New Englanders are characteristically self-reliant, frugal and conservative, particularly when it comes to politics. Their love and respect for their heritage is reflected in the care they take in preserving the rustic simplicity and beauty of their homes and villages, many of them virtually unchanged since Revolutionary times.

The Middle Atlantic States
Of all the sectional groupings in the United States, the Middle Atlantic region has the fewest number of states but perhaps the biggest impact upon the economic, financial and cultural affairs of the country.

The Middle Atlantic States: New York, New Jersey and Pennsylvania, have a combined total land area of 102,745 square miles. They are bordered on the east by New England and the Atlantic Ocean, on the south by the Southern States, on the west by the Midwestern States, and on the north by the Great Lakes and Canada. The topography of the region ranges from a broad coastal plain that fronts on the Atlantic to fertile valleys, rolling plains and the rugged beauty of the Adirondack Mountains in New York State. It also possesses great natural resources in the form of large mineral deposits, extensive wooded areas, highly productive farm land, and an excellent water supply.

Approximately 37 million people, or one out of every six in the nation, live in the region, with about three-quarters of them in cities and suburbs. And, either they or their antecedents have come from one of more than 60 different countries.

From the time the Dutch founded New Netherland, later to be renamed New York by the English, commerce and industry, followed by farming, have been integral to the development of the area. Today, New York City is one of the world's most important port cities, and a center of trade and finance as well as a leader in publishing and the gamut of cultural arts.

During the Revolutionary War, this region was the keystone to the military success of the Americans, with many of the Continental Army's most important battles being fought in the tri-state area. The city of Philadelphia was the seat of the rebellious colonial government, and the birthplace of the Declaration of Independence.

The Southern States

The Southern States, with a combined area of approximately 570,000 square miles, or about one-sixth of the country, complete the eastern seaboard and extend as far west as the boundaries of Texas and Oklahoma. The region includes 14 states, and they, in turn, are split into two subdivisions. Delaware, Kentucky, Maryland and West Virginia are known as "border states" because they lie between the North and the section called the "Deep South". This latter area is made up of the states of Alabama, Arkansas, Florida, Georgia, Louisiana, Mississippi, North Carolina, South Carolina, Tennessee and Virginia.

The topography of the Southern States is comprised of five regions, starting with the Coastal Plain of beaches and marshes that runs from Delaware around the Atlantic shoreline to Louisiana on the Gulf of Mexico. Next, the Piedmont is an area of low hills and upland plains that begins in Delaware, continues down into Alabama and has an abundance of water power to generate electricity. Many of the South's industrial plants, and almost half of its population, can be found in the section known as the Piedmont Industrial Crescent.

West of the Piedmont are the Blue Ridge Mountains, ranging from Maryland to northern Georgia. Then comes the Appalachian Ridge and Valley Region, which also starts in Maryland and runs through Alabama. The iron ore and other raw materials found in this area have made the city of Birmingham, Alabama, one of the major iron and steel centers in the country.

The fifth region, the Appalachian Plateau, can be found in Maryland, West Virginia, Virginia, Tennessee and Georgia. This rough, craggy terrain contains important mineral deposits, especially bituminous (soft) coal.

The South, once totally dependent upon agriculture (cotton, tobacco, rice), now gets most of its income from manufacturing, principally from chemicals, textiles, furniture, wood pulp and paper, lumber and food processing.

Agriculture still has an important role in the economy, however, with well over 1 million farms (about one-third of the U.S. total) in operation. Cotton is the chief income-producing crop, followed by tobacco, peanuts, rice, sweet potatoes, watermelons, tomatoes, peaches and soybeans.

Florida is a leading citrus fruit producer, and Louisiana is just behind Hawaii and California in the production of sugar.

The South, especially West Virginia, has been mining its valuable coal deposits for many years. More recently, gas and oil deposits have been tapped in the Gulf of Mexico off the Louisiana coast.

The Midwestern States

Encompassing one of the richest agricultural regions in the world, and possibly the most productive per acre, the area taken up by the Midwestern States reaches from the Appalachian Mountains in the east to the Rocky Mountains in the west. It stretches as far north as Canada and as far south as the northern border of Arkansas. Twelve states, with a total area of 765,530 square miles (nearly one-fifth of the country), form the mid-section of the United States. They are the main suppliers of food for this country and a substantial number of other parts of the world.

Fertile soil, a comparatively mild climate for most of the area, and a surface that had largely been leveled by glacial action during the Ice Age, have made nearly all the land suitable for raising crops or grazing cattle.

The Midwest has been additionally blessed with an abundance of mineral wealth: iron ore in Minnesota, gold in South Dakota, salt in Michigan, limestone in Indiana, and lead in Missouri. The availability of raw materials and accessibility of an excellent waterway system have enabled Midwesterners to diversify into manufacturing and ship their products all over the world as well as around the country. The St Lawrence Seaway opens the route from the Atlantic to the Great Lakes for ocean-going ships, and vessels in the Lakes can reach the Gulf of Mexico by way of the various tributaries that connect with the Mississippi River.

Approximately 59,000,000 people, about one-quarter of the population of the United States, inhabit the Midwest and produce more food, iron and steel, farm machinery and equipment, transportation equipment, paper, rubber and fabricated metal products than any other section of the country.

The climate varies from the northern states where winters are long and cold with heavy snowfall, and the summers are short, to the southern section where temperatures and length of seasons are just the reverse.

The Southwestern States

No other part of the United States has been as well-publicized or as romanticized as the Southwest. People around the world know about the Southwest in terms of the Hollywood scenario featuring enormous cattle herds, endless vistas, glamorized ranch life, and the All-American folk hero, the cowboy, as personified by John Wayne and Gary Cooper, riding off alone into the sunset.

Some of it is true, of course, but there is a lot more to the Southwest than just cattle, cowboys and scenery.

Four states: Arizona, New Mexico, Oklahoma and Texas, make up the region. The combined area (572,356 square miles) represents about one-sixth of the country, and its total population (21,275,000) adds up to approximately one-eleventh of the nation's people.

The territory extends from the western borders of Arkansas and Louisiana to the southeastern borders of Nevada and California. Mexico is to the south, and the southern borders of Kansas, Colorado and Utah are to the north.

In many ways, the Southwest is a land of contrasts. For example, Santa Fe, New Mexico, dating back to 1610, is the oldest seat of government in the United States, while not too many miles away is Los Alamos, the atomic research center. High-flying jets criss-cross the skies while down below many American Indians still painstakingly work at handicrafts and farming, using the same techniques that their ancestors did hundreds of years ago.

The climate of the Southwest is generally dry, with little humidity, which is the reason for the growth of Phoenix, Tucson and many other communities as winter resorts. The annual average rainfall ranges from five inches in southwestern Arizona to about 50 inches in southeastern Texas. Annual snowfall can be as much as 200 inches in the north-central mountains of New Mexico, but only about one inch in southern Texas and Arizona.

Economically, the area depends on cattle, cotton, citrus fruits, crude oil and copper. Tourism has also become very important, with visitors from all over the country coming to enjoy the climate and see the spectacular sights at the Grand Canyon, the Petrified Forest and the Carlsbad Caverns.

The Rocky Mountain States

United by the rugged, snow-capped spine of rock that stretches from Montana, at the Canadian border, all the way down to New Mexico, the Rocky Mountain region is a study in extremes. The 627,970 square miles covered by six Rocky Mountain states (Arizona and New Mexico are sometimes included in this grouping, but more often are considered Southwestern states, as they have been in this case) represents more than one-fifth of the United States. Yet, fewer people live in this region than in the state of New Jersey, which ranks 46th in size.

The area is boxed in by the Midwestern States on the east, the Southwestern states on the south, the Pacific Coast States on the west, and Canada to the north. The topography includes 1,000 peaks in the Colorado Rockies that measure upward of 10,000 feet in height, Pike's Peak among them. Then, there are the Great Salt Desert in western Utah, more than 4,000 square miles of some of the country's most arid terrain, and Death Valley intruding into southwestern Nevada that lies 282 feet below sea level.

Despite the ranching, mining and lumbering activities that are the economic lifeblood of the region, much of it is still primitive wilderness, with some sections having a population density of less than one person per square mile. This has allowed the region to retain some of the scenic wonders of the nation. Yellowstone National Park along with Zion, Bryce and Hell's Canyon offer some of the most spectacular sights in the world to the thousands of tourists who visit them each year. Yellowstone, the first national park in the U.S., was established in 1872.

The Rocky Mountain region is rich in timber, and minerals like gold, silver, copper, lead, zinc and uranium. In fact, it was the lure of precious metals that brought prospectors into the Rockies and opened the region to settlement. Today cattle raising has surpassed mining and logging, and large numbers of beef cattle, dairy cattle and sheep graze on the wide-open ranges of Montana and Wyoming, making the latter state second only to Texas in the production of wool and sheep.

The natural beauty of their settings plus an abundant snowfall have made places like Aspen and Vail in Colorado, and Sun Valley, Idaho, world famous as winter-resort centers.

The Pacific Coast States

Trying to describe the Pacific Coast States, especially since 1959 when Alaska and Hawaii were included among them, has become an exercise in superlatives.

The combined areas of California, Oregon and Washington, plus the 49th and 50th states, add up to 921,393 square miles, or about one-fourth of the United States. The combined population, 31,799,000, means that about one in every seven Americans lives in these states.

Alaska, the northernmost state, ranks first in size, being almost one-fifth as large as the rest of the United States, and last in population. Hawaii is the southernmost state.

California has the largest population and is third in size. Alaska's Mt McKinley, at 20,320 feet, is the highest peak in the United States, and Death Valley, which stretches along the California-Nevada border is the lowest point in North America.

Alaska has the longest days, up to 20 hours of daylight in summer, which, incidentally, causes its fruits and vegetables to grow to giant size. The state has the widest range of temperatures, registering from -76 degrees Fahrenheit to 100 degrees during the year.

The three conterminous states form the greatest fruit growing region in North America, producing nine-tenths of the pears, one-fourth of the apples, half of the peaches, and one-fourth of the cherries. Most of the nation's prunes, raisins, olives, lemons, filberts, apricots, English walnuts and hops come from this area. The Pacific Coast also contains more than half of the standing commercial timber in the country.

California's San Pedro is the nation's chief fishing port, and the state leads in volume and value of fishery products. It is a foremost producer of oil and natural gas and is sitting on a high percentage of the country's oil reserves.

Most of the planes for the world's commercial airlines are built in either Washington or California, and some of the country's biggest shipyards are on the West Coast.

Last, but not least, the mild climate and beautiful and varied scenery of Southern California have made it the center of the motion picture industry.

That is the story of the United States of America. Fifty states, each with the capability of being an individual and separate entity, yet irrevocably bound together by a shared dream, a common purpose, the pursuit of human dignity, with liberty and justice for all.

Redwood National Park, California.

Above: Gaineswood, Demopolis.

Below: Sturdivant Hall, Selma.

Left: LeRoy Pope House, Huntsville.   Above: Oakleigh, Mobile.   Below: Gorgas House, Tuscaloosa.

Above: Bluff Hall, Demopolis.

Above: Bluff Hall, Demopolis.

Below: Richards-DAR House, Mobile.

Below: Bluff Hall, Demopolis.

Above and below: Richards DAR House, Mobile.

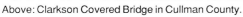Above: Clarkson Covered Bridge in Cullman County.

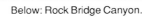Below: Rock Bridge Canyon.

Above: the Natural Bridge of Alabama near Haleyville.

Above: Swann-Joy Covered Bridge, Cleveland.  Below: Rock Bridge Canyon.

Below: DeSoto Falls State Park.

Above: Mobile.

Above: Gaineswood, Demopolis.

Below: the State Capitol Building in Montgomery.

Above: the summit of Cheaha Mountain.

Below: Bellingrath Gardens and Home, near Theodore.

Below: Sturdivant Hall at Selma.

Above: the State Capitol Building in Montgomery.

Below: timbered house in Old North Hull Street Historic District, Montgomery.

Above: townhouse in the Old North Hull Street Historic District, Montgomery.

Below: downtown Mobile.

Above: caribou.

Below: seals in Glacier Bay National Park.

Above: the Mendenhall Glacier.

Above: visitors in Glacier Bay National Park   Below: 4th Avenue in Anchorage.

Above: panning for gold near Fairbanks.   Below: fishermen in the town of Homer.

Below: the Satellite Tracking Station at Gilmore Creek.

Above: Cathedral Park in Juneau.

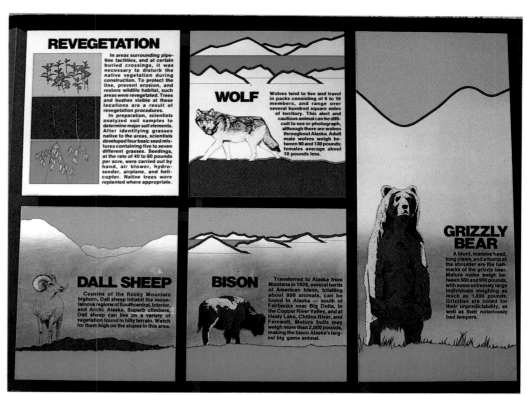

Above: Alaska's wildlife.

Below: Toklat grizzly bear in Denali National Park.

Above: Juneau.

Below: Indian spirit houses at Eklutna.

Below: a disused gold dredge near Fairbanks.

Above: a river gorge near Valdez.

Above: a glacier in the Harding Icefield on the Kenai Peninsula.

Below: the Nenana River in Denali National Park.

Above: pleasure craft on Auke Bay.

Above: boats at their moorings in Seward Marina.

Above: Bright Angel Canyon in the Grand Canyon.

Below: the Grand Canyon at sunset.

Above: the Grand Canyon west of Crystal Rapids.

Above: the Painted Desert.

Below: Tonto National Monument.

Above: cliffs in the Grand Canyon.

Above: the Canyon de Chelly.

Below: the Mitten Buttes in Monument Valley.

Above: Oak Creek Canyon.

Above: the State Capitol in Phoenix.

Below: Tombstone.

Above: Montezuma Castle.

Above: Bonneville, Fort Smith.

Below: Estevan Hall in Helena.

Below: the State Capitol in Little Rock.

Above: Horace Franklin Rogers House, Fort Smith.

Below: farm building near Berryville.

Below: Prairie Grove Battlefield State Park.

Above: Buffalo National River near Harrison.

Below: pasture near Berryville.

Above: Hanging Rock in Sequoia National Park.

Above: Point Lobos.

Below: Death Valley.

Above: a view from the Klamath Overlook.

Below: Redwood National Park.

Above: the Ladybird Johnson Grove of coastal redwoods, Redwood National Park.

Above: the J. Paul Getty Museum.   Below: the Pebble Beach golf course on Monterey Peninsula.

Above: Los Angeles.   Below: Capitol Mall in Old Sacramento

Below: Broad Street in Nevada City.

Below: Los Angeles' Chinatown.

Above: Lombard Street in San Francisco.

Below: Christian Brothers Vineyard near St. Helena.

Above: Mount Shasta.

Below: Fisherman's Village in Marina del Rey.

Below: Grant Avenue in San Francisco's Chinatown.

Above: palm trees in Santa Monica.

Above: the San Francisco-Oakland Bay Bridge across San Francisco Bay.

Below: La Jolla.

Above: Bumpass Hell in Lassen Volcanic National Park.

Below: D.L. Bliss State Park on Lake Tahoe.

Above: Vernal Falls in Yosemite National Park.

General Grant, King's Canyon National Park.

Above: Anza-Borrego State Park.

Below: Monterey Peninsula.

Above: woods around Independence Pass.

Above: Crystal Creek in Gunnison National Forest.

Below: the Sawatch Range and the Twin Lakes on Independence Pass.

Above: downtown Denver.

Below: the Museum of Natural History, Denver.

Below: the State Capitol in Denver.

Above: downtown Denver.

Below: the City and County Building in Denver.

Below: Civic Center Park, Denver.

Below: the Arts Center Mall in Denver.

Above: Maroon Lake.

Above: Deadhorse Mill by Crystal River.

Below: the Great Sand Dunes National Monument.

Above: Rocky Mountain peaks seen from Vail Mountain.

Below: Steamboat ski resort in the Rocky Mountains.

Above: Telluride.

Above: Mystic Seaport.

Below: Madison.

Above: the State Capitol Building in Hartford.

Above: Captain Cove's Marina, Bridgeport.

Above: the harborfront, Bridgeport.

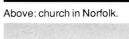
Above: church in Norfolk.　　　　Below: Mystic River.　　　　Right: vessel in Mystic Seaport Museum.

Above: the Congregational Church in Litchfield.

Below: Madison.

Above: vessel in Mystic Seaport Museum.

Below: a covered bridge at West Cornwall.

Below: Noah Webster House in West Hartford.

Above: Davenport College, Yale University, New Haven. Below: Alumni House and Pierson College, Yale. Below: Alumni House, Yale.

Above: the Sterling Memorial Library, Yale.

Below: Alumni House and Pierson College, Yale.

Below: Silliman Campus, Yale.

Above: a farm near Farmington.

Above: the Townsend Building in Dover.

Below: the Capitol Building in Dover.

Above: the United States Capitol in Washington D.C.

Below: the Hirshhorn Museum and Sculpture-Garden, Washington, D.C.

Above: the White House, Washington, D.C.

Above and below: gardens along the Mall, Washington, DC.

Below: gardens along the Mall.

Above: the National Visitors Center, Washington, DC.

Below: Washington Cathedral.

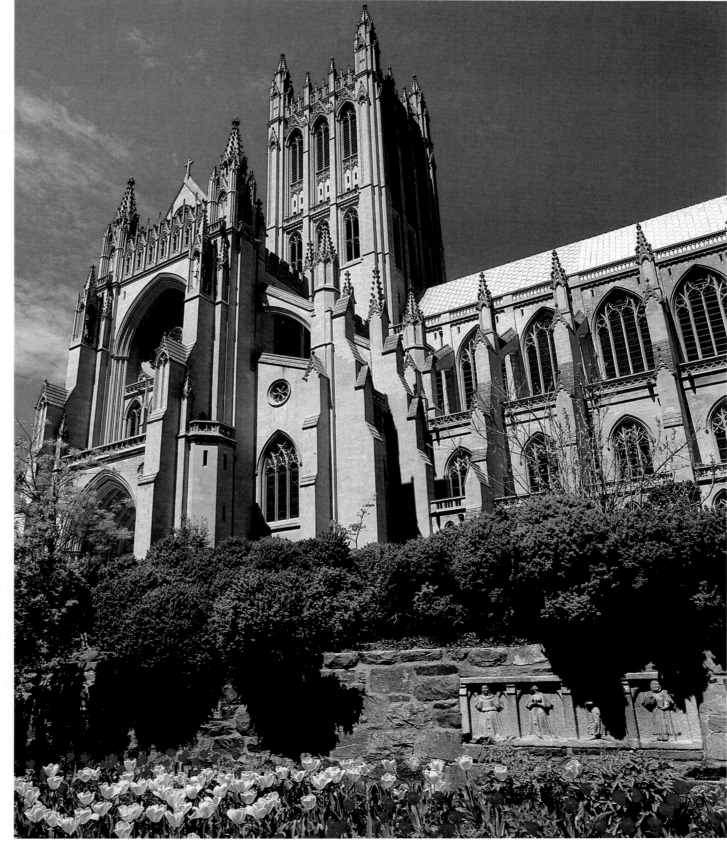

Above: the Smithsonian Institution.

Above: the Library of Congress Building.

Above: Arlington House, the Robert E. Lee Memorial, and Robert F. Kennedy grave.

Below: a marina, Washington, D.C.

Below: Mount Vernon.

Above: the National Air and Space Museum.

Below: Wisconsin Avenue, Georgetown.

Above: the East Building of the National Gallery of Art.

Below: the Library of Congress Building.

Above: the Washington Monument.

Above: Arlington National Cemetery.

Below: the Kennedy Center for the Performing Art

Below: George Washington Masonic National Memorial.

Center left: the Watergate Complex.

Below: a barge on the Chesapeake and Ohio Cana

LET PREJUDICES AND LOCAL INTERESTS YIELD TO REASON.
LET US LOOK TO OUR NATIONAL CHARACTER AND TO THINGS
BEYOND THE PRESENT PERIOD

The GEORGE WASHINGTON
MASONIC NATIONAL MEMORIAL

Above and below: the Vietnam Veterans Memorial, Washington D.C.

Below: the FBI Building, Washington, D.C.

Above: the Hirshhorn Museum and Sculpture Garden.

Below: the Jefferson Memorial, Washington, D.C.

Below: the Bureau of Engraving and Printing, Washington D.C.

Above: the marina, Miami.

Below: Cypress Gardens, near Winter Haven.

Above: Jacksonville.

Above: Mickey Mouse, Walt Disney World.

Above: China, World Showcase, EPCOT Center, Walt Disney World.

Above: dinosaurs, Universe of Energy, EPCOT Center.

Above: Main Street, U.S.A., Walt Disney World.

Below: Contemporary Resort Hotel, Walt Disney World.

Below: Journey into Imagination, EPCOT Center.

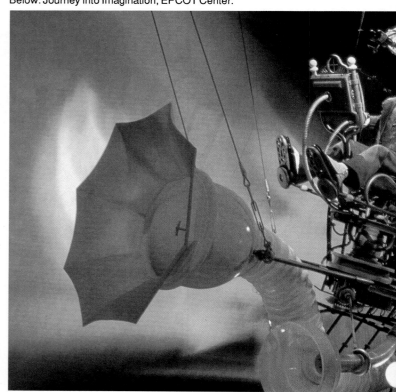

Above: two of the Seven Dwarfs, Walt Disney World.

Above: China, World Showcase, EPCOT Center.

Below: the American Adventure at the EPCOT Center.

Above: Spaceship Earth, EPCOT Center.

Below: Main Street, U.S.A. and Cinderella Castle, Walt Disney World.

Above: Miami Beach.

Below: Daytona Beach.

Above: golf course behind Miami Beach.

Above: Atlanta.

Below: the tomb of Martin Luther King in Atlanta.

Above: the State Capitol Building in Atlanta.

Above: a beach at Savannah.

Below: Fort McAllister.

Above: Stone Mountain.

Above: the Stone Mountain Memorial Carving.

Below: a house in St. Mary's.

Below: Battlefield Park.

Above: Okefenokee State Park.

Below: Andrew Low House in Savannah.

Above: Providence Canyon State Park.

Below: Atlanta University.

Below: St. Simon's Island.

Above: the Governor's Mansion, Atlanta.

Below: a church in St. Mary's.

Below: Fort McAllister.

Above: Kailua Harbor, Hawaii Island.

Below: the Kalalua Valley.

Above: the west coast of Maui at sunset.

Above: Waikiki and Diamond Head on Oahu.

Above: Waikiki Beach, Oahu.

Below: Mauna Lani Bay Hotel, Hawaii Island.

Above: the Hamakua Coast of Hawaii Island.

Below: Sunset Beach, Oahu.

Above: the Koolau Mountains.

Above: the City of Refuge, Hawaii Island.

Above: Fern Grotto near Wailua, Kauai.

Below: Honolulu, Oahu.

Above: the Capitol Building, Boise.

Above: farmland southwest of Boise.

Below: mountains north of Boise.

Above: Burnham Park Yacht Harbor, Chicago.

Above: downtown Chicago.

Below: North Lake Shore Drive, Chicago.

Above: North Lake Shore Drive, Chicago.

Above: the Calder *Red Flamingo* sculpture, Chicago.

Below: Lake Michigan.

Above: the Capitol Building in Indianapolis.

Below: the Indianapolis Motor Speedway.

Above: the Capitol Building, Indianapolis.

Above: Grand Avenue, Des Moines.

Below: Locust Street, Des Moines.

Above: the Capitol Building in Des Moines.

Farmland near Des Moines.

Above and below: farmland in Crawford County.

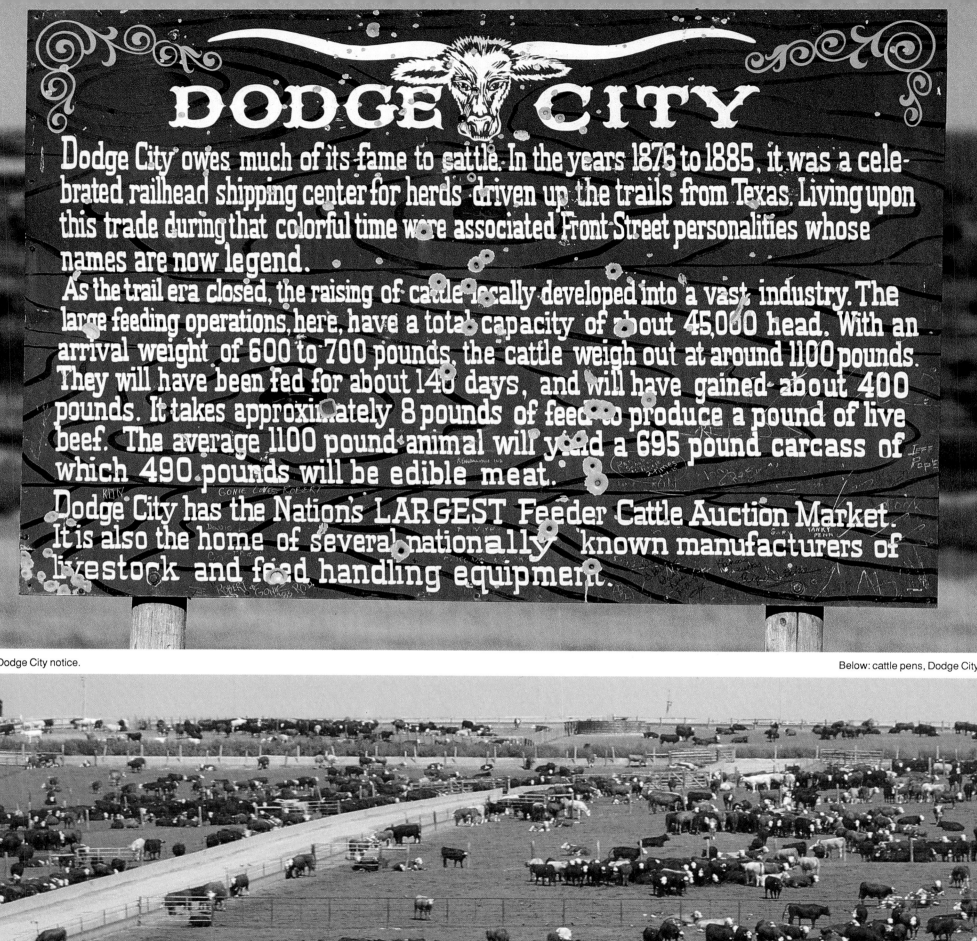

DODGE CITY

Dodge City owes much of its fame to cattle. In the years 1876 to 1885, it was a celebrated railhead shipping center for herds driven up the trails from Texas. Living upon this trade during that colorful time were associated Front Street personalities whose names are now legend.

As the trail era closed, the raising of cattle locally developed into a vast industry. The large feeding operations, here, have a total capacity of about 45,000 head. With an arrival weight of 600 to 700 pounds, the cattle weigh out at around 1100 pounds. They will have been fed for about 140 days, and will have gained about 400 pounds. It takes approximately 8 pounds of feed to produce a pound of live beef. The average 1100 pound animal will yield a 695 pound carcass of which 490 pounds will be edible meat.

Dodge City has the Nation's LARGEST Feeder Cattle Auction Market. It is also the home of several nationally known manufacturers of livestock and feed handling equipment.

Above: Dodge City notice.

Below: cattle pens, Dodge City.

Above: farmland near Wichita.

Above: agricultural land around Wichita.

Above: the Chalk Pyramids at Monument Rocks, south of Oakley.

Below: the State Capitol Building, Topeka.

Above: the sternwheeler *Belle of Louisville* on the Ohio River.

Below: tobacco, west of Lexington.

Below: the Rock Bridge, Red River Gorge.

Above: the U.S. Gold Depository, Fort Knox.

Below: Monument to Zachary Taylor in the National Cemetery, Louisville.

Above: pasture near Danville.

Below: Transylvania University, Lexington.

Below: replica of the original log courthouse in Danville.

Above: a clock in celebration of harness-racing, Louisville.

Above: Cumberland Falls.

Below: Lake Kentucky.

Below: Churchill Downs, Louisville.

Below: the "Old Kentucky Home" of Federal Hill, Bardstown.

Above: the Red Mile Harness Track in Lexington.

Above: a tobacco barn near Frankfort.

Above: Keeneland Horse Sale.

Below: Almahurst Farm near Lexington.

Above: horses in the bluegrass country of the Lexington plain.

Below: the Red Mile Harness Track in Lexington.

Above: Mardi Gras in New Orleans.

Below: downtown New Orleans.

Above: the Vieux Carré, New Orleans.

Above: Oak Alley Plantation at Vacherie.

Above: Ardoyne, near Houma.

Above: North Monmouth.

Below: sunrise from the top of Mount Cadillac.

Above: Bass Harbor Light on Mount Desert Island.

Above: fishing quays near Pemaquid Point.

Above: Boothbay Harbor.

Below: Pemaquid Lighthouse.

Above: Boothbay Harbor.

Above: Friendship.

Below: Port Clyde.

Above: Stonington, on Deer Isle.

Below: Maine sunset.

Above: Port Clyde.

Above: a lake near Southwest Harbor, Mount Desert Island.

Below: Park Loop Road in Acadia National Park, Mount Desert Island.

Above: rocks on the southeast shoreline of Mount Desert Island.

Above: the United States Naval Academy at Annapolis.

Below: Baltimore.

Above: Annapolis.

Above: the dome of the State House, Annapolis.

Above: Inner Harbor, Baltimore.

Below: a house on Main Street, St. Michaels.

Below: Baltimore City Hall.

Below: Sotterly, Hollywood.

Above: Charles Street and the Washington Monument, Baltimore.

Below: the Benjamin Stevens House in Easton.

Below: Hammond-Harwood House, Annapolis.

Above: Inner Harbor, Baltimore.

Below: Annapolis.

Below: Washington St., Easton.

Below: a replica of the *Dove*.

Above: Main Street in St. Michaels.

Below: the Power Plant on Inner Harbor, Baltimore.

Below: the Maritime Museum in St. Michaels.

Above: Inner Harbor, Baltimore.

Below: Annapolis.

Below: Paca House, Annapolis.

Above: Provincetown.

Below: Mill Creek Marsh at Sandwich.

Above: Massachusetts fishing quays.

Above: Nauset Beach, Cape Cod.

Below: Provincetown.

Above: Gayhead Cliffs, Martha's Vineyard.

Above: the State House, Boston.

Above: Longfellow House, Cambridge.

Below: North Bridge, Concord.

Above: Old Sturbridge Village.   Below: Hawkes House, Salem.

Above: Sankaty Head Lighthouse.   Below: Cape Cod.

Below: Pickering Wharf, Salem.   Below: Boston.

Above: Rockport.

Below: a barn in Hancock Shaker Village.

Above: *USS Constitution*, Boston.

Below: *Beaver II*, Boston Tea Party Museum.

Below: Fairhaven.

Above: the John Hancock Tower in Boston.

Below: Boston skyscrapers and the dome of the State House.

Above: Beacon Hill, Boston.

Above: the Renaissance Center in Detroit.

Below: the lighthouse at Point Betsie.

Above: Upper Herring Lake, near Frankfort.

Above: Sault Ste. Marie on the St. Lawrence Seaway.

Below: the Houghton Hancock Bridge.

Above: the Renaissance Center, Detroit.

Above: Fort Michilimackinac.

Below: the Coast Guard Station at Marquette, on Lake Superior.

Above: the pier and lighthouse at Grand Haven.

Above: the Baptism River.

Above: Split Rock Lighthouse.

Below: a creek near Split Rock.

Above: Nicollet Mall, Minneapolis.

Below: 3rd Avenue Buildings overlooking Government Center Plaza, Minneapolis.

Below: the Seventh Place shopping mall, Saint Paul.

Above: the Landmark Center in Saint Paul.

Below: Minneapolis.

Below: Marquette Avenue, Minneapolis.

Above: the Gooseberry River.

Above: Saint Paul.

Below: the lighthouse at Grand Marais.

Above: Nicollet Mall, Minneapolis.

Above: the Riverplace restaurant, Minneapolis.

Below: Minnesota State Office Building, Saint Paul.

Above: modern building near Peavey Plaza, Minneapolis.

Below: downtown Minneapolis.

Above: the Foshay Tower, Minneapolis.

Above: Orchestra Hall, Minneapolis.

Below: City Hall and Government Center Plaza, Minneapolis.

Above: cotton growing in Coahoma County.

Below: Moon Lake.

Above: Desoto Lake.

Above: the Charles McLaran House, Riverview, in Columbus.

Above: Glen Auburn, Natchez.

Below: Longwood, Natchez.

Above: the water mill in Grand Gulf Military Monument Park.

Above and below: Vicksburg National Military Park.

Above: Vicksburg National Military Park.

Below: the Shirley House, Vicksburg National Military Park.

Below: a derelict church at Grand Gulf.

Above: a memorial in Vicksburg National Military Park.

Above: Vicksburg National Military Park.

Above and below: Vicksburg National Military Park.

Above: the "Widow Blakely", Vicksburg.   Below: Vicksburg National Military Park.

Below: Vicksburg National Military Park.

Above: Dawt Mill.

Left: a pumpkin figure near Sibley.   Above: Alley Springs Mill.   Below: Appleton Mill.

Above: the City Market, Kansas City.

Above: corn-harvesting.

Above: Dillard Mill.

Below: Alley Springs Mill.

Below: Ballinger Mill.

Above: Ravenswood House near Tipton.

Below: Vaille Mansion, Kansas City.

Above: Kansas City Museum.

Above: the Old Courthouse, St. Louis.

Below: the Giralda Tower, Kansas City.

Below: St. Charles County Courthouse.

Below: the Gateway Arch, St. Louis.

Above: Jesse Hall, University of Missouri, Columbia.

Below: Rockcliffe Mansion.

Below: the State Capitol Building, Jefferson City.

Above: the Gateway Arch, St. Louis.

Above: tobacco-curing barn near Weston.

Below: the home of Mark Twain, Hannibal.

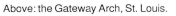

TOM SAWYERS FENCE
HERE STOOD THE BOARD
FENCE WHICH TOM SAWYER
PERSUADED HIS GANG TO
PAY HIM FOR THE PRIVILEGE
OF WHITEWASHING TOM
SAT BY AND SAW THAT IT
WAS WELL DONE

Below: the Meramec Caverns near Stanton.

Below: cattle farming.

Above: Tom Sawyer and Huckleberry Finn, Cardiff Hill.

Below: the Mississippi near Hannibal.

Above: dark Montana mountains.

Below: Swiftcurrent Lake in Glacier National Park.

Above: Garden Wall above McDonald Creek.

Above: Virginia City.

Above: Virginia City.

Above: saloon, Virginia City.

Above and below: Virginia City.

Below: Virginia City.   Below: Virginia City.

Above: branding on the Padlock Ranch, Bear Creek.

Left: roundup on the Padlock Ranch.

Above: branding on the Padlock Ranch.

Below: repairing fences on the Padlock Ranch.

Above: Padlock Ranch horses.

Below: Padlock Ranch cowboys.

Above: branding at the Padlock Ranch.

Below: cattle on the Padlock Ranch.

Above and below: farmland west of Ogallala.

Above: Chimney Rock, southeast of Scotts Bluff.

Above and below: rodeo in Gordon, Sheridan County.

Above: rodeo in Gordon, Sheridan County.

Above: Omaha.

Below: the Scouts Rest Ranch in the Buffalo Bill State Historical Park.

Above: Scotts Bluff National Monument.

Above: a casino in Stateline.

Above: Fremont Street, Las Vegas.

Below: Lake Tahoe.

Above: Virginia City.

Below: a casino in Stateline.

Above: Virginia City.	Below: a casino in Stateline.

Above: Lake Tahoe.

Above and below: the Ponderosa Ranch, Incline Village.

Above and below: the Ponderosa Ranch.

Below: Virginia City.

Below: the Ponderosa Ranch.

Below: the Ponderosa Ranch.

Above and below: restored Virginia City.

Below: a hotel bar, Virginia City.

Below: Virginia City.

Above: Virginia City.   Below: the Fourth-Ward School, Virginia City.   Above: Bucket of Blood Saloon, Virginia City.

Above: dead wagon, Virginia City.   Below: Virginia City.

Above: the Cog Railway on Mount Washington.   Below: Echo Lake near North Conway.

Right: Whitneys Inn at Jackson.

Above: snow in the White Mountains.

Below: Portsmouth.

Below: Mt. Washington Hotel, Bretton Woods.

Above: White Mountain National Forest.

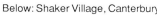

Above: a forest home at Jackson.

Below: Glen Ellis Falls.

Right: the Union Church, Stark.

Above: a house in the central White Mountains.

Below: Attitash ski resort.

Below: Barret House, New Ipswich.

Above: the Swift River near Conway.

Below: a lighthouse near Portsmouth.

Below: the Rocky Gorge Scenic Area.

Above: Leamings Run botanical gardens at Swainton.

Below: Mantoloking.

Above: pier at Ocean Grove.

Above: Princeton University.   Below: the Palmer Stadium, Princeton.   Above: Atlantic City.

Below: Atlantic City.   Below: Oyster Creek near Leeds Point.

Below: farm buildings in the south.

Above: Manasquan.

Below: Cape May.

Below: Wildwood, near Cape May.

Below: harness racing.

Above: farmland near Trenton airfield.

Above: a farm at Newton.

Below: Spring Lake.

Above: the church of San Felipe de Neri in Albuquerque.

Below: the Mission of San Miguel.

Above: Pueblo de Taos.

Above: Gila National Forest.

Below: Shiprock, San Juan County.

Above: rock formations in the Carlsbad Caverns.

Above: boats moored in Montauk.

Below: Jones Beach on the Atlantic Ocean.

Above: Jones Beach.

Above: Van Cortlandt Manor at Croton-on-Hudson.

Above: Van Buren House, Kinderhook.

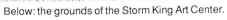

Below: the grounds of the Storm King Art Center.

Below: re-enactment of the Battle of Stony Point

Center right: General Patton, West Point.

Below: Van Cortlandt Manor at Croton-on-Hudson.

Above: Niagara Falls. Below: New Windsor Cantonment

Below: the Capitol Building, Albany.

Below: Thayer Hall

Above: the Financial District of New York.

Below: Central Park. Below: Manhattan.

Above: Turtle Bay in the East River. Below: Manhattan.

Below: South Street Seaport.

Above: mill at Philipsburg Manor, North Tarrytown.

Below: the house on Washington Irving's estate.

Above: the Hudson River near Hyde Park.

Below: General Knox's HQ at the New Windsor Cantonment.

Above: the Vanderbilt Mansion.

Below: the Hudson River at Rhinecliff.

Below: Rip Van Winkle Bridge near Catskill.

Below: the Empire State Plaza and the Capitol, Albany.

Above: the Home Moravian Church, Old Salem.

Below: a farm near Raleigh.

Above: hot-air ballooning

Above: Tannahill, Wilmington.

Below: Orton Plantation near Wilmington.

Above: a house on Forest Hills Drive, Wilmington.

Below: Airlie Gardens near Wilmington.

Above: Cape Hatteras Lighthouse.

Above: Biltmore House.

Below: a view from the Blue Ridge Parkway, south of Asheville.

Above: a farm near Berthold.

Below: an oil well near Tioga.

Above: farmland east of Williston.

Above: Cincinnati.

Below: the port of Toledo on Lake Erie.

Above: a bridge at Seven Caves near Bainbridge.

Above: Highway 75 crossing the Ohio in Cincinnati.

Below: the Arcade, Cleveland.

Above: the Ohio River.

Above: Central Bridge, Cincinnati.

Above: Lucas County Building, Toledo.

Below: Portside, Toledo.

Below: Central Bridge, Cincinnati.

Above: Clifton Mill.

Above: Hyde Park Medical Arts Building, Cincinnati.

Below: the Williamstown Bridge across the Ohio.

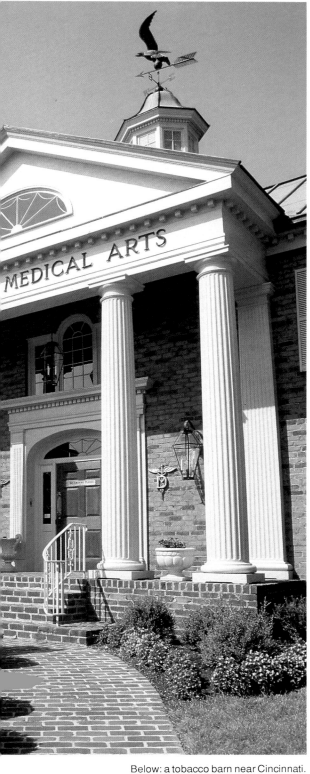

Above: Hawthorn Hill.

Below: a cornfield in western Ohio.

Below: a tobacco barn near Cincinnati.

Below: the State Capitol Building.

Below: Tyler Davidson Fountain, Cincinnati.

Above: horses grazing near Sallisaw.

Below: City of Faith Medical Center, Tulsa.

Above: stockyard, Oklahoma City.

Below: the Blue Ribbon Down Race Track near Sallisaw.

Above: the Arkansas River, Tulsa.

Above: Indian powwow, Tulsa.

Below: National Cowboy Hall of Fame, Oklahoma City.

Above: Boulder Park.

Below: the Kiamichi River near Rattan.

Above: grounds of Philbrook Art Center.

Below: the State Capitol, Oklahoma City.

Below: Philbrook Art Center.

Above: sculpture outside the Tulsa Performing Arts Center.

Above: Robert S. Kerr Park, Oklahoma City.

Above: Robert S. Kerr Park, Oklahoma City.

Below: Park Avenue, Oklahoma City.

Below: Woodward Park.

Below: Myriad Gardens, Oklahoma City.

Above: highway at Stanfield.
Above: Oneonta Gorge.

Below: the Oregon Dunes National Recreation Area.

Below: Cannon Beach.

Below: Cannon Beach.

Below: farm buildings near the South Umpqua River.

Above: Mount Hood beyond Trillium Lake.

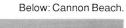

Below: basking Steller sea lions.
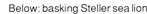

Above: Portland.

Below: Washington Park.

Above: Morrison Street, Portland.

Above: the State Capitol Building in Salem.

Below: Pioneer Courthouse Square, Portland.

Above: Yaquina Bay Bridge, Newport.

Below: Eugene.

Above: Harris Beach State Park.

Above: Samuel Boardman State Park.

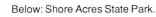

Below: Shore Acres State Park.

Below: Crater Lake.

Above: Multnomah Falls in the Cascade Range.

Above: Hells Canyon on the Snake River.

Below: the Oregon Dunes National Recreation Area.

Below: the botanical gardens in Shore Acres State Park.

Above: the view west from near Crater Lake.

Below: Sunrise Lodge, Bachelor Mountain Ski Area.

Above: a covered bridge at Washingtonville.

Below: Lancaster County.

Above: farmland in Lancaster County.

Above: the Monongahela River, Pittsburgh.

Below: the Allegheny Center and the clocktower of Carnegie Free Library, Pittsburgh.

Above and below: Pittsburgh.

Below: the Gateway Clipper Station on Monongahela River, Pittsburgh.

Below: PPG Place, Pittsburgh.

Below: Robert Indiana's "Love" sculpture, Philadelphia.

Above: Carpenters' Hall, Philadelphia.

Below: City Hall, Philadelphia.

Below: the USS Olympia, Penns Landing, Philadelphia.

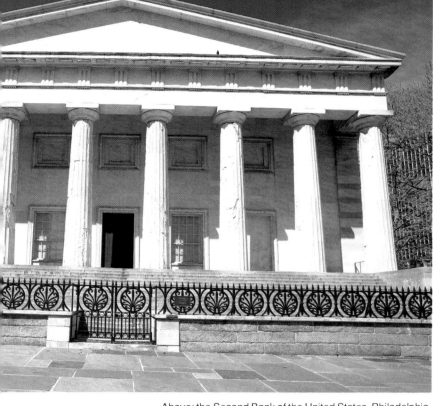

Above: the Second Bank of the United States, Philadelphia.

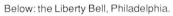

Above: Penn's Landing, Philadelphia.

Below: the Liberty Bell, Philadelphia.

Below: Chinatown, Philadelphia.

Above: the First Bank of the United States, Philadelphia.

Below: the Museum of Art, Philadelphia.

Above and below: Gettysburg National Military Park.

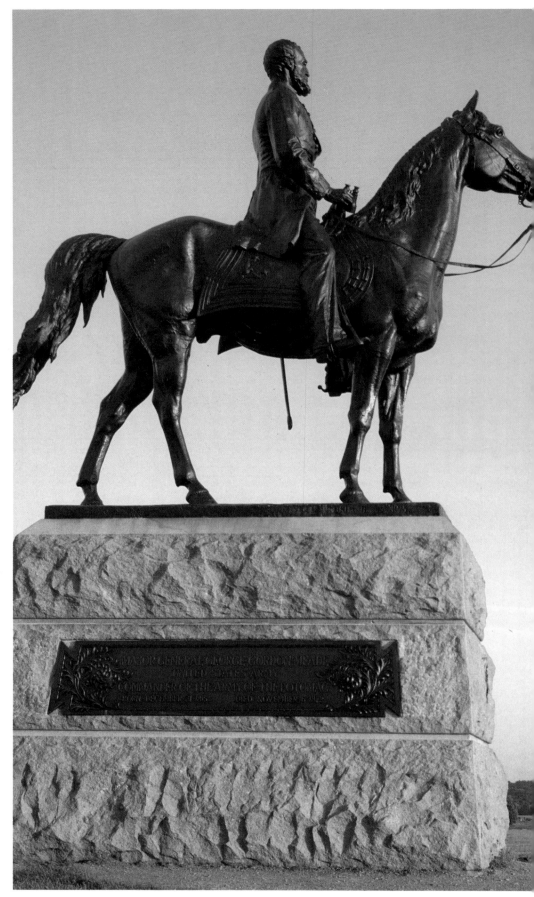

Above and below: Gettysburg National Military Park.

Above: the Headquarters of the Army of the Potomac.

Above and below: Gettysburg National Military Park.

Above and below: Gettysburg National Military Park.

Above: farm, Gettysburg.

Below: Gettysburg National Military Park.

Above: the State House, Providence.

Below: Newport Casino.

Above: Newport sailing regatta.

Below: Thames Street, Newport.

Below: Château-sur-Mer.

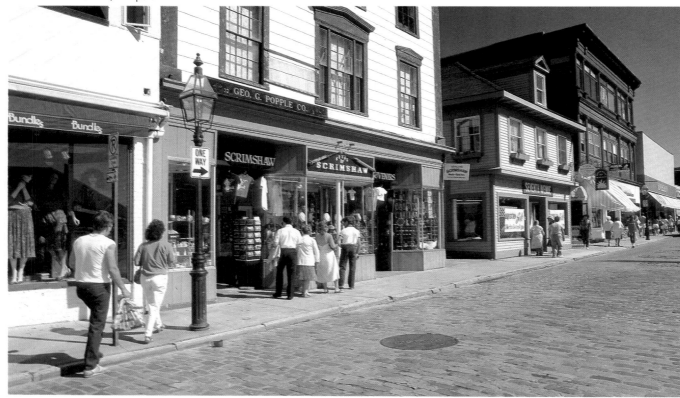

Above: Bowen's Wharf, Newport.

Below: Newport Bridge.

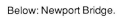

Above: Newport.

Below: Trinity Church, Newport.

Above: Newport viewed from the east.

Above: the Old Colony House, Newport.

Below: Brown University, Providence.

Above: a beach near Misquamicut.

Below: Bellevue Avenue, Newport

Below: fishing boats, Narragansett.

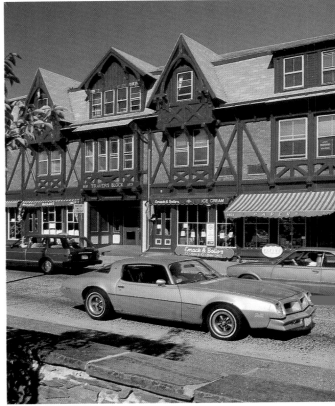

Below: Misquamicut.

Below: Point Judith Lighthouse.

Below: Misquamicut.

Below: Cornelius Vanderbilt's The Breakers, Newport.

Below: Newport Bridge.

Above: the Wedge Plantation near Charleston.

Above and below: Cypress Gardens.   Above: Rose Hill Plantation.

Above: Lake Keowee.

Above: Rutledge Avenue overlooking Colonial Lake.

Above: St. Michael's Episcopal Church, Charleston.

Below: Battery Park, Charleston.

Below: Greenville's Freedom Week Aloft.

Below: Battery Park, Charleston.

Below: Edisto Beach.

Above: Wagon Train Compound, Custer State Park.

Below: farmland off Interstate 90.

Above: River Valley Cedar Pass in Badlands National Park.

Above: the Interstate 40 bridge across the Wolf River.

Below: the reconstruction of Fort Loudon, Vonore.

Above: Boynton Park, Chattanooga.

Above: the Old Mill at Pigeon Forge.

Below: Graceland, Memphis.

Below: the Victorian Village District, Memphis.

Below: Jonesboro. Above: the Little River, Smoky Mountains.

Below: the Stones River National Battlefield, Murfreesboro.

Above: Chimney Tops in the Smoky Mountains.

Below: view from the Morton Overlook.

Above: a stream near Greenbrier in the Smoky Mountains.

Below: the Little River in the Smoky Mountains.

Below: a black bear, Smoky Mountains.

Above: the Guadalupe Mountains.

Below: Enchanted Rock State Natural Area.

Above: El Capitan in Guadalupe Mountains National Park.

Above: Old Fort Parker State Historic Site.

Above: the Chapel of Presidio Santa Maria del Loreto de la Bahia.

Above: the Governor's Mansion, Austin.

Below: Manor Downs, Austin.

Above: El Paso.

Below: oil derrick off Galveston.

Below: Old City Park Museum, Dallas.

Above: Yellow House in Rockport.

Below: downtown San Antonio.

Below: Santa Elena Canyon.

Below: a pier off Seawall Boulevard, Galveston.

Above: the Texas State Capitol, and the First Methodist Church, in Austin.

Above: the Alamo Chapel, San Antonio.

Below: Mission Concepcion in San Antonio.

Above and below: La Rosita Ranch at Eagle Pass.

Below: cutting sick calves from the bunch, La Rosita Ranch.

Above: La Rosita Ranch, Eagle Pass.

Below: the X Ranch at Kent.

Above: La Rosita Ranch, Eagle Pass.

Above: fishing off Corpus Christi.

Below: Interstate Highway 35 south of San Antonio.

Above: Corpus Christi Marina.

Above: downtown Houston.

Below: the Wortham Fountains in Tranquility Park, Houston.

Above: the Sweeney Clock on Bagby Street, Houston.

Below: modern sculpture at the InterFirst Plaza, Houston.

Above: downtown Houston.

Below: the Houston Center, Houston.

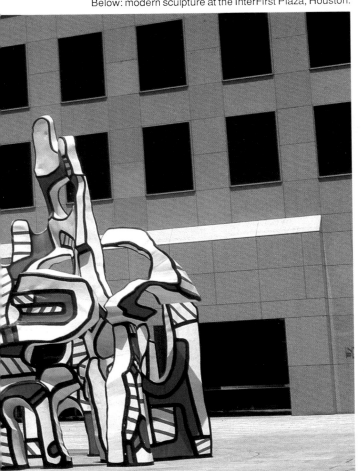

Above: the Texas Stadium at Irving.

Below: Main Street, Fort Worth.

Above: the Reunion Tower, Dallas.

Above: the Sentinel in Zion National Park.

Below: Double Arch, Arches National Park.

Above: the Watchman in Zion National Park.

Above: Bryce Canyon National Park, Utah.

Below: Paria View, Bryce Canyon National Park.

Above: the Fairyland Trail, Bryce Canyon National Park.

Above: farm buildings near Rutland.

Below: horses in the village of Peru.

Above: Mount Ethan Allen.

Above: a house in Shelburne.

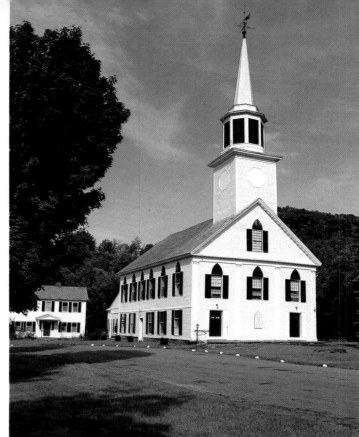

Above: a church in Townsend.

Below: Mount Mansfield ski area.

Below: a house in Woodstock.

Above: Middletown Springs.   Below: Quechee Falls.

Above: winter landscape.   Below: Grafton.   Below: a church at Poultney.

Above: the State House in Montpelier.

Below: Windham Cottage in Grafton.

Above: West Danville and Joe's Pond.

Below: Grafton.

Below: Vermont College in Burlington. Below: Equinox Valley Nursery near Manchester.

Above: a covered bridge in the Shenandoah Valley.

Below: "Stonewall" Jackson, Monument Avenue, Richmond.

THE LINCOLN GUN

CAST IN 1860, THIS WAS THE FIRST 15-INCH RODMAN GUN. ITS RANGE WAS MORE THAN FOUR MILES. WEIGHT OF THE PROJECTILE WAS OVER 300 LBS. DURING CIVIL WAR IT WAS USED TO BOMBARD CONFEDERATE BATTERIES ON SEWELLS POINT. THE GUN WAS NAMED FOR PRESIDENT LINCOLN IN MARCH 1862.

STONEWALL JACKSON

Above: the Lincoln Gun, Fort Monroe.   Below: Virginia Beach, Ocean Front.   Below: Petersburg National Battlefield.

Above: Washington Street, Alexandria.

Above: King Street, Alexandria.

Above: Moore House, Yorktown.

Below: Norfolk.

Above: St. Mark's Episcopal Church, Richmond.

Below: crabs at Crisfield.

Above: Chatham Manor near Fredericksburg.

Below: Ash Lawn garden, Charlottesville.

Left: Sherwood Forest.   Above: Ash Lawn, Charlottesville.   Below: Monticello, Charlottesville.

Above: Monticello, Charlottesville.

Below: Mount Vernon.

Below: Oatlands, near Leesburg.

Above: the State Garrison Regiment and Williamsburg Militia celebrate July 4, Market Square.

Below: "Volley of Joy" fired by musketeers on July 4, Colonial Williamsburg.

Above: the Governor's Palace, Colonial Williamsburg.

Right: the Magazine, Colonial Williamsburg.

Below: the Governor's Palace, Colonial Williamsburg.

Above and below: Berkeley Plantation near Williamsburg.

Right: Norfolk Botanical Gardens.

Above: Seattle.

Below: the Space Needle, Seattle.

Above: Mount Shuksan.

Above and below: Palouse farming country.

Above: coastal forest.

Above: Rialto Beach.

Below: the Palouse River.

Above: Glacier Peak in the Cascade Mountains.

Above: Seattle.

Below: the Space Needle, Seattle.

Above: Mount Adams beyond Takhlakh Lake.

Above: Harpers Ferry in the Blue Ridge Mountains.

Below: the Shenandoah River at Harpers Ferry.

Above: the railroad bridge at Harpers Ferry.

Above: Harpers Ferry footbridge, Blue Ridge Mountains. Below: Shenandoah National Park Headquarters, Virginia. Below: a farm, Harpers Ferry.

Above: the railroad bridge at Harpers Ferry.

Below: Harpers Ferry.

Above: wild lupins north of Washburn.

Below: frozen marshes on the shores of Lake Superior near Port Wing.

Above: the Capitol Building, Madison.

Above: Lakeside Park, Milwaukee.

Above: Bayfield on Lake Superior.

Below: a road near Eau Claire.

Above: Minerva Terrace at Mammoth Hot Springs, Yellowstone National Park.

Below: Castle Geyser, Yellowstone National Park.

Above: Jackson Lake in the Grand Teton Mountains.

Above: the Shoshone River.

Above: Mount Moran beyond Oxbow Bend.

Below: the Snowy Mountains.

Above and below: the Grand Tetons.

Above: the Snake River in Grand Teton National Park.

Above: Grand Teton.

Above: the Grand Tetons.

Below: the Snake River at Oxbow Bend.

ALABAMA

Bellingrath Gardens and Home, Theodore 31
Bluff Hall, Demopolis 27
Cheaha Mountain 30
Clarkson Covered Bridge, Cullman County 28
DeSoto Falls State Park 28
Gaineswood, Demopolis 26, 30
Gorgas House, Tuscaloosa 26
LeRoy Pope House, Huntsville 26
Mobile 30, 31
Montgomery 30, 31
Natural Bridge of Alabama 28
Oakleigh, Mobile 26
Richards-DAR House, Mobile 27
Rock Bridge Canyon 28, 29
Sturdivant Hall, Selma 26, 30
Swann-Joy Covered Bridge, Cleveland 29

ALASKA

Anchorage 34
Auke Bay 38
Eklutna 35
Gilmore Creek 34
Glacier Bay National Park 32, 34
Harding Icefield, Kenai Peninsula 37
Homer 34
Juneau 35
Lake Hood 38
Mendenhall Glacier 33
Nenana River, Denali National Park 37
Seward Marina 39

ARIZONA

Canyon de Chelly 44
Grand Canyon 40, 41, 43
Montezuma Castle 47
Monument Valley 44
Oak Creek Canyon 45
Painted Desert 42
Phoenix 46
Tombstone 46
Tonto National Monument 42

ARKANSAS

Bonneville, Fort Smith 48
Buffalo National River 49
Estevan Hall, Helena 48
Horace Franklin Rogers House, Fort Smith 48
Little Rock 48
Prairie Grove Battlefield State Park 49

CALIFORNIA

Anza-Borrego State Park 61
Christian Brothers Vineyard, St. Helena 55
Death Valley 51
D.L. Bliss State Park, Lake Tahoe 58
Fisherman's Village, Marina del Rey 55
J. Paul Getty Museum 54
King's Canyon National Park 60
Klamath Overlook 52
La Jolla 57
Lassen Volcanic National Park 58
Los Angeles 54
Monterey Peninsula 54, 61
Mount Shasta 55

Nevada City 54
Old Sacramento 54
Point Lobos 51
Redwood National Park 52, 53
San Francisco 55, 57
Santa Monica 56
Sequoia National Park 50
Yosemite National Park 59

COLORADO

Crystal Creek, Gunnison National Forest 63
Deadhorse Mill 67
Denver 64, 65
Great Sand Dunes National Monument 67
Maroon Lake 66
Rocky Mountains 68
Sawatch Range 63
Steamboat ski resort 68
Twin Lakes 63
Telluride 69

CONNECTICUT

Bridgeport 72
Hartford 71
Litchfield 73
Madison 70, 73
Mystic River 72
Mystic Seaport 70, 72, 73
Noah Webster House, West Hartford 73
Norfolk 72
West Cornwall 73
Yale University, New Haven 74, 75

DELAWARE

Capitol Building, Dover 77
Townsend Building, Dover 77

DISTRICT OF COLUMBIA

Arlington House, Washington, D.C. 82
Arlington National Cemetery, Washington, D.C. 84
Bureau of Engraving and Printing, Washington D.C. 85
Chesapeake and Ohio Canal 84
FBI Building, Washington, D.C. 85
Georgetown 82
George Washington Masonic National Memorial, Washington, D.C. 84
Hirshhorn Museum and Sculpture-Garden, Washington, D.C. 78, 85
Jefferson Memorial, Washington, D.C. 85
Kennedy Center for the Performing Arts, Washington, D.C. 84
Library of Congress Building, Washington, D.C. 82, 83
Mall, Washington, D.C. 80
Mount Vernon 82
National Air and Space Museum, Washington, D.C. 83
National Gallery of Art, Washington D.C. 83
National Visitors Center, Washington, D.C. 81
Smithsonian Institution 82
United States Capitol, Washington D.C. 78
Vietnam Veterans Memorial, Washington D.C. 85
Washington Cathedral 81
Washington Monument, Washington, D.C. 84
Watergate Complex, Washington, D.C. 84
White House, Washington, D.C. 79

FLORIDA

Cypress Gardens, Winter Haven 86
Daytona Beach 90
Jacksonville 87
Miami 86
Miami Beach 90, 91
Walt Disney World 88, 89

GEORGIA

Andrew Lowe House, Savannah 96
Atlanta 92, 93, 97
Atlanta University 97
Battlefield Park 96
Fort McAllister 94, 97
Okefenokee State Park 96
Providence Canyon State Park 97
St. Mary's 96, 97
St. Simon's Island 97
Savannah 94
Stone Mountain 95, 96

HAWAII

City of Refuge, Hawaii Island 104
Fern Grotto, Kauai 105
Hamakua Coast, Hawaii Island 102
Honolulu, Oahu 105
Kailua Harbor, Hawaii Island 98
Kalalua Valley 98
Koolau Mountains 103
Maui 99
Mauna Lani Bay Hotel, Hawaii Island 101
Sunset Beach, Oahu 102
Waikiki, Oahu 100, 101

IDAHO

Boise 106

ILLINOIS

Burnham Park Yacht Harbor, Chicago 108
Chicago 109, 110, 111
Lake Michigan 111

INDIANA

Indianapolis 112, 113

IOWA

Crawford County 117
Des Moines 114, 115

KANSAS

Dodge City 118
Kansas City 121
Monument Rocks 121

KENTUCKY

Almahurst Farm, Lexington 126
Belle of Louisville, Ohio River 122
Cumberland Falls 125
Churchill Downs, Louisville 124
Danville 124
Keeneland Horse Sale 127

Lake Kentucky 125
Louisville 124
Old Kentucky Home, Federal Hill, Bardstown 125
Red Mile Harness Track, Lexington 126, 127
Rock Bridge, Red River Gorge 122
Transylvania University, Lexington 124
U.S. Gold Depository, Fort Knox 123
Zachary Taylor Monument, Louisville 123

LOUISIANA

Ardoyne 131
New Orleans 128, 129
Oak Alley Plantation, Vacherie 130

MAINE

Acadia National Park 138
Bass Harbor Light, Mount Desert Island 133
Boothbay Harbor 134, 135
Friendship 135
Mount Cadillac 132
Mount Desert Island 138, 139
North Monmouth 132
Pemaquid Lighthouse 134
Port Clyde 135, 137
Stonington, Deer Isle 136

MARYLAND

Annapolis 141, 142, 144, 145
Baltimore 140, 142, 143, 144, 145
Benjamin Stevens House, Easton 143
Easton 144
Hammond-Harwood House, Annapolis 143
Paca House, Annapolis 145
St. Michaels 142, 144
Sotterly, Hollywood 142
United States Naval Academy, Annapolis 140

MASSACHUSETTS

Boston 150, 152, 153, 154, 155
Cape Cod 152
Fairhaven 153
Gayhead Cliffs, Martha's Vineyard 149
Hancock Shaker Village 153
Hawkes House, Salem 152
Longfellow House, Cambridge 151
Nauset Beach, Cape Cod 148
North Bridge, Concord 151
Old Sturbridge Village 152
Pickering Wharf, Salem 152
Provincetown 146, 148
Rockport 153
Sandwich 146
Sankaty Head Lighthouse 152

MICHIGAN

Detroit 156, 159
Fort Michilimackinac 160
Grand Haven 161
Houghton Hancock Bridge 158
Marquette, Lake Superior 160
Point Betsie 156
Sault Ste. Marie 158
Upper Herring Lake 157

MINNESOTA

Baptism River 162
Gooseberry River 166
Grand Marais 167
Minneapolis 164, 165, 168, 169
Saint Paul 164, 165, 167, 168
Split Rock Lighthouse 163

MISSISSIPPI

Charles McLaran House, Columbus 172
Coahoma County 170
Desoto Lake 171
Glen Auburn, Natchez 173
Grand Gulf Military Monument Park 174
Longwood, Natchez 173
Moon Lake 170
Vicksburg National Military Park 174, 175

MISSOURI

Alley Springs Mill 176, 177
Appleton Mill 176
Ballinger Mill 177
Dawt Mill 176
Dillard Mill 177
Jefferson City 179
Jesse Hall, University of Missouri, Columbia 179
Kansas City 178
Mark Twain home, Hannibal 180
Meramec Caverns 180
Mississippi River 181
Ravenswood House, Tipton 178
Rockcliffe Mansion 179
St. Louis 178, 180
St. Charles County Courthouse 178
Vaille Mansion, Kansas City 178

MONTANA

Garden Wall 183
Padlock Ranch, Bear Creek 186, 187
Swiftcurrent Lake, Glacier National Park 182
Virginia City 184, 185

NEBRASKA

Chimney Rock 189
Gordon, Sheridan County 190, 191
Omaha 192
Scotts Bluff National Monument 193
Scouts Rest Ranch, Buffalo Bill State Historical Park 192

NEVADA

Lake Tahoe 194, 195
Las Vegas 194
Ponderosa Ranch, Incline Village 195
Stateline 194, 195
Virginia City 194, 195, 196, 197

NEW HAMPSHIRE

Attitash ski resort 204
Barret House, New Ipswich 204
Cog Railway, Mount Washington 198
Echo Lake, North Conway 198
Glen Ellis Falls 202

Mt. Washington Hotel, Bretton Woods 200
Portsmouth 200
Rocky Gorge Scenic Area 205
Shaker Village, Canterbury 201
Stark 203
Swift River 205
White Mountains 200
White Mountain National Forest 201
Whitneys Inn, Jackson 199

NEW JERSEY

Atlantic City 208
Cape May 209
Leamings Run botanical gardens, Swainton 206
Manasquan 209
Mantoloking 206
Ocean Grove 207
Oyster Creek 208
Palmer Stadium, Princeton 208
Princeton University 208
Spring Lake 211
Wildwood 209

NEW MEXICO

Albuquerque 212
Carlsbad Caverns 215
Gila National Forest 214
Mission of San Miguel 212
Pueblo de Taos 213
Shiprock, San Juan County 214

NEW YORK STATE

Albany 219, 223
Hudson River 222, 223
Jones Beach 216, 217
Montauk 216
New Windsor Cantonment 219, 222
New York 220, 221
Niagara Falls 219
Philipsburg Manor, North Tarrytown 222
Rip Van Winkle Bridge 222
Storm King Art Center 218
Thayer Hall 219
Van Buren House, Kinderhook 218
Van Cortlandt Manor, Croton-on-Hudson 218
Vanderbilt Mansion 223
Washington Irving's estate 222
West Point 218

NORTH CAROLINA

Airlie Gardens 227
Biltmore House, Asheville 229
Cape Hatteras Lighthouse 228
Old Salem 224
Orton Plantation 226
Tannahill, Wilmington 226

NORTH DAKOTA

Farmland 230, 231

OHIO

Cincinnati 232, 234, 235, 236, 237
Cleveland 234
Clifton Mill 236
Columbus 237
Hawthorn Hill 237
Ohio River 234
Seven Caves 233
Toledo 232, 235
Williamstown Bridge 236

OKLAHOMA

Arkansas River 238
Blue Ribbon Down Race Track 238
Boulder Park 239
City of Faith Medical Center, Tulsa 238
Kiamichi River 239
Oklahoma City 238, 240, 241
Philbrook Art Center 240
Tulsa 240
Woodward Park 240

OREGON

Bachelor Mountain Ski Area 249
Cannon Beach 242, 243
Crater Lake 247
Eugene 245
Harris Beach State Park 247
Hells Canyon, Snake River 248
Mount Hood 243
Multnomah Falls, Cascade Range 248
Oneonta Gorge 242
Oregon Dunes National Recreation Area 242, 248
Portland 244
Salem 245
Samuel Boardman State Park 246
Shore Acres State Park 246, 248
Yaquina Bay Bridge, Newport 245

PENNSYLVANIA

Gettysburg National Military Park 256, 257
Headquarters of the Army of the Potomac 257
Lancaster County 250, 251
Philadelphia 254, 255
Pittsburgh 252, 253

RHODE ISLAND

Breakers, Newport 263
Brown University, Providence 262
Château-sur-Mer 258
Misquamicut 262, 263
Narragansett 262
Newport 258-263
Newport Bridge 259, 261, 263
Point Judith Lighthouse 263
Providence 258

SOUTH CAROLINA

Charleston 266, 267
Cypress Gardens 265
Edisto Beach 267
Lake Keowee 266
Rose Hill Plantation 265
Wedge Plantation 264

SOUTH DAKOTA

Badlands National Park 271
Custer State Park 268
Lake Oahe 270
Mount Rushmore 269

TENNESSEE

Boynton Park, Chattanooga 273
Chimney Tops, Smoky Mountains 276
Fort Loudon, Vonore 272
Graceland, Memphis 274
Interstate 40 bridge 272
Jonesboro 275
Little River, Smoky Mountains 275, 277
Memphis 274
Pigeon Forge 274
Smoky Mountains 276, 277
Stones River National Battlefield, Murfreesboro 275

TEXAS

Alamo Chapel, San Antonio 283
Austin 282
Corpus Christi 287
Dallas 280, 291
El Paso 280
Enchanted Rock State Natural Area 278
El Capitan, Guadalupe Mountains National Park 279
Fort Worth 290
Galveston 281
Governor's Mansion, Austin 280
Guadalupe Mountains 278
Houston 288, 289
Interstate Highway 35, San Antonio 286
La Rosita Ranch, Eagle Pass 284, 285
Manor Downs, Austin 280
Mission Concepcion, San Antonio 283
Old Fort Parker State Historic Site 280
Presidio Santa Maria del Loreto de la Bahia 280
San Antonio 281
Santa Elena Canyon 281
Texas Stadium, Irving 290
X Ranch, Kent 285
Yellow House, Rockport 281

UTAH

Arches National Park 292
Bryce Canyon National Park 294, 295
Zion National Park 292, 293

VERMONT

Equinox Valley Nursery 301
Grafton 299, 300
Middletown Springs 299
Montpelier 300
Mount Ethan Allen 297
Mount Mansfield ski area 298
Poultney 299
Quechee Falls 298
Shelburne 298
Townsend 298
Vermont College, Burlington 301
West Danville 301
Woodstock 298

VIRGINIA

Alexandria 303
Ash Lawn, Charlottesville 304
Berkeley Plantation 308
Chatham Manor 304
Colonial Williamsburg 306, 307
Fort Monroe 302
Moore House, Yorktown 303
Monticello, Charlottesville 304, 305
Mount Vernon 305
Norfolk 303
Norfolk Botanical Gardens 309
Oatlands 305
Petersburg National Battlefield 302
Richmond 302, 303
Shenandoah National Park Headquarters 320
Shenandoah Valley 302
Sherwood Forest 304
Virginia Beach, Ocean Front 302

WASHINGTON

Glacier Peak, Cascade Mountains 315
Mount Adams 317
Mount Shuksan 311
Palouse 312
Palouse River 314
Rialto Beach 314
Seattle 310, 316

WEST VIRGINIA

Harpers Ferry, Blue Ridge Mountains 318, 319, 320, 321
Shenandoah River 318

WISCONSIN

Bayfield, Lake Superior 325
Lakeside Park, Milwaukee 324
Lake Superior 322
Madison 323

WYOMING

Castle Geyser, Yellowstone National Park 326
Grand Teton 332
Grand Tetons 330, 333
Jackson Lake, Grand Teton Mountains 327
Mammoth Hot Springs, Yellowstone National Park 326
Mount Moran 329
Shoshone River 328
Snake River, Grand Teton National Park 331, 333
Snowy Mountains 329